Housing for Life

Housing for Life
A guide to housing management practices

Christine Davies

*Former principal lecturer in Housing
Sheffield Polytechnic*

With contributions by

Jane Darke
Ian Cole and **Kath Windle**

E & FN SPON
An Imprint of Chapman & Hall
London · New York · Tokyo · Melbourne · Madras

**Published by E & FN Spon, an imprint of Chapman & Hall,
2–6 Boundary Row, London SE1 8HN**

Chapman & Hall, 2–6 Boundary Row, London SE1 8HN, UK

Van Nostrand Reinhold Inc, 115 5th Avenue, New York NY10003, USA

Chapman & Hall Japan, Thomson Publishing Japan, Eirakawacho
Nemoto Building, 6F, 1-7-11 Hirakawa-cho, Chiyoda-ku, Tokyo 102,
Japan

Chapman & Hall Australia, Thomas Nelson Australia, 102 Dodds Street,
South Melbourne, Victoria 3205, Australia

Chapman & Hall India, R. Seshadri, 32 Second Main Road, CIT East,
Madras 600 035, India

First edition 1992

© 1992 Christine Davies

Typeset on 10/12 Times by Graphicraft Typesetters Ltd, Hong Kong
Printed in Great Britain by Page Bros., Norwich

ISBN 0 419 12070 X   0 442 31510 4 (USA)

A catalogue record for this book is available from the British Library

Library of Congress Cataloging-in-Publication data available

To all those relatives and friends who thought that I would never finish it!

Contents

Contributors

Christine Davies is a researcher and housing consultant. From 1972–1989, she was a Principal Lecturer on housing policy and administration at Sheffield City Polytechnic. Prior to lecturing, she was Director of a local authority housing department, having worked in a number of local authorities and housing associations.

Ian Cole is Principal Lecturer in Housing and Head of the Housing Division in the School of Urban and Regional Studies at Sheffield City Polytechnic. He was Director of the Housing Decentralisation Research Project from 1987 to 1989. He is currently undertaking research on tenure change, housing and state welfare and housing education.

Jane Darke has been researching, teaching and writing about housing for several years. She has worked in housing management with two inner city local authorities and now teaches at Sheffield City Polytechnic.

Kath Windle is Senior Research Officer in the Housing Research Section of Sheffield City Council. She was Research Associate in the Housing Decentralisation Research project from 1987 to 1989.

Preface

In many housing organizations housing management has been practised in a paternal and complacent fashion. There have been pockets of innovation and an awareness of the desires and needs of tenants, but it is the present Conservative government's legislation which is speeding the forces for change. Housing professionals in local authorities and housing associations are becoming increasingly aware of the necessity for changes in approach and the need to manage such change. Managements who do not respond will pay the price in loss of tenant loyalty, funding and staff demoralization. This is not to say that the government's legislation is entirely desirable — most is disastrous for those people in greatest need — but one of the side effects has been to sharpen housing management response.

One of the major difficulties in the area of housing is an inherent tension between the political agenda of governments and the practical needs of organizations and the people they serve. Housing resources, the functions of housing departments and statutory duties are all dictated by central government. On many occasions the practical housing needs of individuals will be circumscribed by the political needs of a given party in power.

This political tension is exacerbated by the financial constraints placed on housing organizations by central government leading to conflict. On one hand organizations are being told to be economic, efficient and effective and work within cash limits. On the other hand the people for whom the organizations exist are given rights and have expectations which cannot be met within the resources available. The recent analysis of the housing service in local authorities by the Audit Commission concentrates on the financial efficiency of those organizations leaving the resource question as a political decision. This concentration on finance is at the expense of the organization's social responsiveness and accountability to the population who are in need of housing. The phrase 'equal opportunity for all' has a hollow ring in the housing field.

The idea of tension between the political, organizational and personal levels is implicit in this book. *Housing for Life* represents a credo which regards the needs of the person seeking help as paramount. Housing is needed for life, but at different times of life the need will be different. Trying to meet each household's need is a challenge demanding ingenuity, flexibility and imagination.

The organization of this book makes explicit the tension between the organizational principles of the housing service and the experience of the people using it.

A second theme is the understanding of the interdependence of all aspects of housing despite inherent conflicts. Increasingly the lines between public and private sectors are becoming blurred and this encourages less-blinkered solutions. Co-operation must also extend to other professions and organizations, particularly with the introduction of community care and organization concerned with the housing for special groups.

There have been few textbooks written on housing management. The most comprehensive is Mary Smith's *Guide to Housing*, which is very wide ranging, taking in policy and management. The Housing Research Group of the City University published *Could local authorities be better landlords?*, Allen and Unwin published Anne Power's book *Property before People* and Macmillan published *Housing Associations: Policy and practice* by Helen Cope, which covers the voluntary sector. The latter two are based on research work in local authorities. Most housing management information is in a welter of reports, research papers, magazine articles, single chapters in books and single-topic booklets. The constant stream of legislation also requires the re-writing of so much material that a great deal becomes dated very quickly. This book attempts to draw together published information on basic texts and give further reading which will be useful to housing students and interested practitioners.

The book is divided into two parts. The first part consists of three chapters relating to overall management and the second part of three chapters relating to particular themes, described in detail below.

Chapter 1 provides an overview of management change in the past two decades, looking at re-organization of the authorities, the rise of the voluntary sector, fashions in management and why it has all happened. This sets the context for Chapters 2 and 3 which concentrate on organization and equal opportunities. Chapter 2 summarizes the theoretical context for management, and then discusses the example of decentralization as a response to tenants' complaints against the rigidity of the bureaucracy. Chapter 3 looks at equal opportunities in aspects of service delivery and employment. A growing number of organizations are taking action in this area and this chapter draws together key issues which should be given priority in organizations.

The second part of the book looks at a housing history of typical clients and examines the options open to them. The pattern of the chapters is to take a current management issue, state the legal situation, follow the housing history of the typical client and consider housing solutions.

Chapter 4 describes delivery of services and reviews the chances of an elderly woman tenant of a local authority to move to sheltered housing. The existing service and her alternatives are considered followed by speculation about her future if further care is needed. Chapter 5 introduces homelessness and looks at a single black woman who leaves home after a row, becomes pregnant, suffers harassment and who then has to experience the weary round of hostels etc. before eventually obtaining a permanent home. Equally, this profile serves for young men as the options that are open to them are very similar, but there is an extra dimension to womens' needs by the very fact of being a woman. Chapter 6 is devoted to tenant participation in housing through following the fortunes of a husband and wife and two children moving from private rented property to a housing association home with the opportunity to have a say in its design. Later they become involved in a tenant co-operative.

It has to be remembered that there are many other types of households, such as larger families, lesbian and gay, brothers and sisters, inter-generation and group living. Many of the solutions discussed will be applicable to such households, but there is scope for another book to pursue the particular needs and management issues involved in providing housing for them.

It is hoped that students and interested practitioners will gain knowledge on basic housing management practices and a feeling for an approach which puts the needs of the home hunter first.

My thanks must go to colleagues who have contributed to the book; Jane Darke, Ian Cole and Kath Windle for all their work. Thanks must also be given to friends, colleagues and ex-students who have commented on and contributed ideas to the book. In particular I would like to thank Colin Foster, for taking time from a busy period to read chapters and comment and to Derek Burns for useful editing and moral support. Finally, the publishers should receive a medal for patience.

Abbreviations

AC	Audit Commission
ADC	Association of District Councils
AMA	Association of Metropolitan Authorities
CHAC	Central Housing Advisory Committee
CHAR	Housing Campaign for Single Homeless People
CRE	Commission for Racial Equality
DOE	Department of the Environment
DSS	Department of Social Security
EOC	Equal Opportunities Commission
GLC	Greater London Council
HAG	Housing Association Grant
HAT	Housing Action Trust
HMO	House in Multiple Occupation
HRA	Housing Revenue Account
IOH	Institute of Housing
LGTB	Local Government Training Board
LSE	Leasehold Schemes for the Elderly
MBO	Management by Objectives
NCC	National Consumer Council
NFHA	National Federation of Housing Associations
PEP	Priority Estate Project
TMC	Tenant Management Co-op
TPAS	Tenant Participation Advisory Service

Part One

Overall Management

1

Overview of the organization of housing services

1.1 Introduction

An overview is presented of the continuing pressures on the management of housing over the past two decades and the responses to those pressures by the housing profession. Subsequent chapters amplify the particular aspects of decentralization; equal opportunities; quality of service; homelessness and tenant participation.

The role of the housing service in both local authorities and the voluntary sector is undergoing an intense period of change. In local authorities this change has been forced by a combination of legislation passed by a government which no longer subscribes to the provision of housing by authorities and the changing social attitudes and aspirations of the people needing housing. There is also a questioning of the effectiveness, efficiency and economy of the service, and whether it can be done better by other means (Audit Commission, 1986). However, there is a danger that in the drive to promote such financial objectives, considerations of equity and equality for all consumers will be lost. A balance must be struck.

The role of government is central. As a result of reduced finance, authorities are being forced to encourage other agencies to meet housing need and to act as a co-ordinator of services. Central Government wishes to see this enabling role extended. However, authorities differ widely in size, type of stock, political approaches and their local community needs. This means that there can never be a standard solution. Some authorities will try to divest themselves of their properties via local authority housing associations; only a small number have done this so far. Others will instead seek to become more people-oriented by listening to the wishes of the community and improving their services accordingly.

The housing service in the voluntary sector is also changing. It is expected to pick up the role of provision of housing for low-income groups but using private funds. This is causing tensions in the voluntary movement, for most housing associations were set up and are run by committed people with an interest in providing housing for specific groups at 'reasonable' rents and filling gaps in local authority provision. The legislative changes are forcing a new role on associations, often at odds with their constitutions and the wishes of their committees. Some of the bigger associations are, however, embracing the new regime.

All these changes demand a new organizational and management approach from housing staff but there is no single body of work which sets out specific theories for them to follow. It can be argued that it does not lend itself to this being based on procedures and precedents which have grown up over time. On the other hand attempts have been made to apply general management models, for example, corporate planning. These to a considerable extent have failed (Clapham, 1985/86). There is, however, a growing body of empirical research on how housing organizations are actually structured and managed (Glasgow University, 1989; Kirby, Finch and Wood, 1988; City University, 1981; Niner, 1989; Audit Commission, 1986; Welsh Office, 1989). In addition the Audit Commission (AC), the Local Government Training Board (LGTB) and the National Federation of Housing Associations (NFHA) have published advice and research not only on good management techniques, but also raising concerns about the future. Such research is a necessary preliminary to producing effective advice on management styles and practices. A useful discussion paper is *A new management for housing departments* (Stewart, 1988) which speculates on the future direction for local authority departments. The voluntary movement has tried to direct associations into better management by, for example, the publication *Standards for Housing Management* (NFHA, 1987) which is used as a basis for monitoring by the Housing Corporation.

The use of the phrase 'housing services' is deliberately applied to public and voluntary sectors, for in the direct management of tenants in homes a service-centred approach should be used by all housing organizations.

The other pressures for change have built up over a period of about twenty years. Local authorities, in the early sixties, were small and concerned with the detail of local services. At that time there were a series of reports on the re-assessment of the role of local government, which coupled with major social changes in attitudes and life styles, and the rise of activist participation led to demands from the public for improved services. These combined pressures resulted in a major re-organization of local authorities in the United Kingdom in the following years:

- 1965 in London;
- 1971 in Northern Ireland (the Northern Ireland Housing Executive was set up to replace the local authorities);
- 1974 in England and Wales;
- 1975 in Scotland.

Housing associations were also subject to change in this period. They were traditionally mainly philanthropic with a few newer and marginally more commercial ventures. The National Federation of Housing Societies (NFHS) began to encourage associations to expand from simple low cost housing to providing sheltered housing for the elderly and special provision for the handicapped. Alongside this expansion into special need areas, associations were drawn into the wider field of provision by the Housing Act 1964 which introduced loans for 'cost rent housing', (i.e. homes rented on a non-profit basis). The success of a pilot scheme administered by the NFHS led to the government establishing the Housing Corporation under the Housing Act 1961 to encourage special types of associations to provide houses and flats to be let at cost rents or for ownership by the occupiers (Smith, 1989). The 1974 Housing Act led to further expansion by introducing a financial framework for housing associations. There was a focus on specialist needs which was felt to complement the local authorities' provision.

Central Government has called into question the favourable grant system to the associations. The Housing Corporation is, therefore, urging associations to reduce the proportion of grant in their schemes and increase private funding. The ethos of associations is beginning to change to a more commercial outlook, and organizational change is concomitant.

All this does not mean there is one 'best' style of management, the Glasgow University research team (1989) found in England that 'Organisational type or structure is not the key determinant of effectiveness, nor indeed is the difficulty of the context managed. What matters most is the will to manage efficiently and effectively'. This gives a fillip to the supporters of public housing in that there is considerable sense in local authorities still providing housing with a differing management approach. A similar finding was reported in the Welsh Office study (1989).

The remainder of this chapter will provide an overview of the organization of housing services, including a review of factors affecting them over a period of time, management model fashions, techniques for managing change and some speculation about the future.

1.2 Reasons for change since 1969

Four reasons for change have been suggested and are listed below. They will be discussed in turn.

1. Influence of government reports.
2. Social change.
3. Rise of participation.
4. Political ideology.

1.2.1 Influence of Government Reports

The major organizational changes from this direction have been in the local government arena. After the implementation of the 1974 Housing Act, housing associations have had to cope with the problems of growth but have not been subject to a welter of investigations and reports.

Prior to 1974 local authorities ran their affairs through a series of committees and departments, bounded by professional interests such as the Town Clerk, the Treasurer, the Engineer, the Public Health Inspector. Heads of housing departments were not always Chief Officers and there was not necessarily even a separate department, despite the urgings of the Central Housing Advisory Committee (CHAC) and its influential Cullingworth Committee Report (1969). The decision to review the system of local government was not single or deliberate; it just grew. Various reports were published under governments of differing persuasions. Lord Redcliffe-Maud, and Wood (1974) expressed this in stating:

> the one common thread running through the decisions to examine this or that aspect of local government was simply the alleged inadequacy of the system to cope with the growing demands made on it as governments continued to extend the range of public services and as conditions of daily life were transformed by the increasing mobility and size of the population.

The following reports are the most relevant to local government housing matters prior to 1974:

- 1960 Royal Commission on Local Government in Greater London. Cmnd. 1164 (Herbert Report);
- 1967 Report of the Committee on the staffing of Local Government (Mallaby Report);
- 1967 Report of the Committee on the Management of Local Government (Maud Report);
- 1968 Report of the Committee on Local Authority and Allied Personal Services. Cmnd. 3703 (Seebohm Report);
- 1969 Royal Commission on Local Government in England. Cmnd. 4040 (Redcliffe-Maud Report);

- 1972 The New Local Authorities: Management and structure. DOE (Bains Report).

These independent Royal Commissions and Committees reviewed the workings of local government culminating in the Local Government Act of 1972. This Act set up a permanent Boundary Commission and the new structure of local government, which of course affected the structure of housing departments. The Bains Report (1972) published guidelines for the new authorities to follow, although these could not be made mandatory as the democratically elected authorities managed their own business.

Many authorities followed the Bains line, creating new committee structures and directorates. The intention was to produce a structure which cut across narrow professional boundaries and encouraged the taking of 'corporate decisions'. Housing as a multi-disciplinary service lends itself to this concept and has been incorporated into a variety of structures. It may be a separate department, it may be in an environment directorate combining public health, parks, engineers and housing, or it may be part of the social services department. The committees responsible for the work of these departments will vary too, sometimes combining the work of several departments or of just a single one. The wide variety of structures has resulted partly from a genuine attempt to impose some corporate logic on an entrenched bureaucracy, and partly from past power struggles of committee members, chief officers and the advice of management consultants. Despite the advice of so many CHAC reports, particularly the Cullingworth report, Table 1.1 (p. 6) will give some idea of how far the ideal of a comprehensive housing department eludes the profession.

When reports affecting associations are looked at the picture is slightly different. The major reports are:

- 1965 Report of the Committee on Housing in Greater London. Cmnd. 2605 (Milner Holland Report);
- 1971 Housing Associations. A working paper of the CHAC. A summary of evidence (Cohen report);
- 1976 DOE Final Report of the Working Party on Housing Co-operatives (Campbell Report);
- 1985 Housing co-ops — After ten years. H. Campbell;
- 1985 The Evidence. Inquiry into British Housing (HRH Duke of Edinburgh Report).

These Reports, plus the White Papers Fair Deal for Housing (1971) and Widening the Choice: Next Steps in Housing (1973), discussed the role of housing associations and co-operatives rather than their structural and organizational matters. Financial support from both Conservative and Labour governments ensured that the voluntary movement grew. It is the growth factor,

Table 1.1 Housing functions most commonly carried out in local authorities by departments other than housing

Function	% in other departments
Housing benefits payments to private sector tenants	67
Carrying out repairs	66
Computer services	59
Housing benefit payments to council tenants	55
Performance review	44
Rent accounting	40
Rent collection	31
Repair administration	29
Sales to sitting tenants	28

Source: Table 2.2 in The Nature and Effectiveness of Housing Management in England, Glasgow University, Centre for Housing Research. (1989). With the permission of the Controller of HMSO.

with its attendant escalating costs, which has highlighted the need for effective and efficient management. The annual reports of the Housing Corporation show that 1561 new associations were registered in 1975/76, growing to 2632 by 1983/84 and numbers have not increased significantly since then. Table 1.2 details the numbers of properties which have been built and rehabilitated by housing associations in Great Britain. It shows how investment has declined drastically in the last five years.

The way housing associations have been structured has been partly the work of the Corporation and partly the work of the NFHA. Most housing management and development advice has come from the latter. It has also acted as a negotiating body with the Housing Corporation for the movement as a whole.

As a result of re-structuring in local authorities, housing became the major function of the new District Councils. Housing Committees gained greater status and this reflected on the work of the housing staff. Central government was still committed to funding the building and rehabilitating of homes and gave responsibility to Housing Committees for vast sums of money. The housing profession was, therefore, given an opportunity to enhance its professional status.

1.2.2 Social change

The changes in the social patterns of living have been striking in the past two decades. There are two major factors here, numbers and attitudes. There

Table 1.2 Numbers of completed new build and rehabilitated properties by Housing Associations

Year	Great Britain	England	Wales	Scotland
79/80	24 086	20 693	1534	1859
80/81	30 693	25 956	1173	3564
81/82	26 448	20 014	2328	4106
82/83	26 899	21 637	2115	3147
83/84	26 869	20 658	1535	4676
84/85	30 817	25 335	1487	3995
85/86	25 272	21 329	1520	2423
86/87	24 173	19 981	1424	2766
87/88	22 867	18 183	1767	2917
88/89	17 890	13 238	1662	2990

Source: Adapted from the annual reports of the Housing Corporation (1979/80 to 1988/89).

are an increasing number of households being formed out of separations, divorce and young people leaving home earlier. In addition the people at the peak birth rate born in the early sixties are setting up home, as are heterosexual or homosexual couples or friends deciding to share a home. There is also a growth in the number of elderly, particularly those over 75 years, who need smaller and more convenient homes. Finally, the recognition of the existence of a growing number of vulnerable people in society, plus the policy of closing long-stay hospitals and returning people to the community, is putting additional demands on housing provision.

These demographic changes are accompanied by three attitude changes. Personal aspirations are said to be geared towards owner occupation (BSA, 1983). It is common sense to want to own when the financial advantage is weighed towards ownership rather than renting. Nevertheless, the 35% who must rent or wish to, also want a reasonable deal, with good provision and services.

With widespread unemployment and oppressive interest rates, the percentage of those who rent is unlikely to decrease. Tenants are becoming aware of their rights as enacted in the Housing Acts of 1980, 1985 and 1988 and the Housing and Planning Act 1986 makes it mandatory for them to be informed by their landlord of these.

Within the generality of tenants there is a significant number of black and ethnic minority groups whose voice is growing louder. Increasingly there is a recognition that Britain has become a multi-racial and multicultural society and that discrimination must be eliminated. Gender issues are also gaining recognition as there is a growing awareness that a high proportion of the homeless are one parent families most of whom are headed by women (see

Chapter 3 for gender and race issues). Housing organizations are in a unique position to take a lead in ensuring that their tenants are treated fairly in a central part of their lives, namely their home.

All these issues put pressure on the management skills of housing staff and demand a wider range of solutions than in the past. It is no longer enough to set a target for building specific types of houses and flats. Housing users need different solutions at different times of their lives and are expressing these demands in their refusal to accept poor housing.

1.2.3 The rise of participation

From the sixties onwards a range of political forces, such as the environmental and ecology organizations, womens' movement, black groups, squatter groups and campaigners in the inner city have developed the ideas 'of greater personal and popular control over key political and social decisions' (Beuret and Stoker, 1986). Many political activists blooded in the 1960s' resistance to wholesale clearance of old housing (Dennis, 1972) and the disintegration of communities in the inner cities, graduated to become councillors. The infusion of new ideas and people into local government has created, in a limited number of authorities, a climate for change which has allowed tenant participation and self management to develop. However, the spread of such ideas has been slow, with the larger authorities dictating the pace. Decentralization is often the chosen method.

Some housing associations established after 1974 were pioneered by similarly-committed political activists wishing to involve tenants in running their own affairs. Examples are Circle 33 in London and North Sheffield Housing Association. Others continued to provide a service to tenants which bordered on the paternalistic. The NFHA has taken a lead in encouraging these latter associations to examine their management ethos and ensure that tenant participation becomes a reality.

As an alternative to taking the services to the tenants there is the further possibility of them running their own affairs by using the legislation to set up management co-operatives (Housing and Planning Act, 1986). The co-operative takes over the management functions of the local authority or housing association under a management agreement, excluding rent setting. In effect the co-operative becomes the landlord's agent but has no stake in the equity. There have been limited numbers to date but they have been relatively successful. There is further discussion of this in Chapter 6.

These initiatives have been introduced by the landlord. In the past, tenants often set up associations in answer to a grievance. Nevertheless many of these progressed, along with the newer sort of associations, to become a representative force with members sitting on sub- and main-housing committees and in certain cases having the right to vote (Craddock, 1975). This right has been abolished by the terms of the Local Government and Housing Act

1989, Part 1. This is sad, for evidence given to the Inquiry into British Housing (NFHA, 1986) by two tenant organizations made it clear that there was a need for a consumer voice in housing and for the funding of independent tenants' organizations. In some cities the tenants' associations have formed a federation and are supported by grants from the local authority. In Sheffield, three pence a week is set aside from each rent to subsidise the tenants' associations and the development work carried out by the federation; individual tenants may opt out. Tenants have set up a National Tenants Organization which has international links, and more recently the National Tenants and Residents Organization has been established.

Since the introduction of the tenants' right to consultation in 1980 and the right to 'opt out' in the Housing Act 1988, tenants have been in need of good impartial advice. The Tenant Participation Advisory Service (TPAS) offers that advice, and influences how housing organizations approach the consultation and participation process. In addition, a number of housing consultancies have sprung up to advise both landlords and tenants. Even the Housing Corporation has established posts for tenants' advisors who will ensure that tenants wishing to transfer from local authorities to associations will be properly informed. Grants are available under the Housing and Planning Act 1986 s.16 and the Housing Acts 1985 s.87 and 1988 s.50. The pressure from all these sources has increased the awareness of both Authority and Association landlords that services to tenants must improve.

1.2.4 Political ideology

The last reason for change is perhaps the most potent. In the 1987 White Paper entitled Housing: The Government's Proposals (1987 CM214) the government has declared its aim of increasing ownership, giving public tenants a greater choice of landlord, and improving the efficiency and effectiveness of local authorities. Legislation since 1980 has been aimed at encouraging the sale of council homes and manipulating the transfer of others to alternative landlords. This has been achieved through a mixture of financial carrots to the tenants in the form of discounts and a financial stick to the authorities in the form of cash limits. However, the legislation has only been partially successful. Sales of Council houses and flats have levelled off with just over a million being sold (Social Trends, 1989). The transfer of tenants to other landlords has been mostly vetoed by the tenants themselves. By June 1991 only fourteen authorities have been able to transfer properties to housing associations. The threat of losing stock and being financially squeezed has led authorities to critically examine their management practices, financial control and general performance. To ensure that tenants vote to remain with the local authority an effort has been mounted to consult, inform and improve services. From the research conducted by Glasgow University (1989) it is clear that authorities are rising to the challenge. For example, the national postal survey found that almost a third of the large councils had introduced neighbourhood offices and that 67% of council tenants were satisfied with the service they received.

The report also showed that housing associations too are not immune from financial constraints and need to consult tenants to improve management policies. The Government expects the voluntary movement to expand its building programme and take over council homes where tenants wish it. To cope with the possibility it behooves them to ensure that their management practices are at least equal in quality to those of authorities, and this must be demonstrated to new tenants. However, funding does not match the legislative intent, and many associations are not geared up to suddenly manage a larger number of homes. Additionally the NFHA has called on associations not to poach local authority tenants unless requested to do so by the tenants, and in many areas informal agreements exist between authorities and associations to this effect.

It is clear from the Glasgow University research that both Authorities and Associations face similar management problems, operating in difficult neighbourhoods with poor and dependent households. The myth of poor local authority management and effective caring housing associations has no basis. 'Good management performance and low cost were not the preserve of a single organisational type' (Glasgow, 1989). Unfortunately the myth was used as fuel for the legislative changes, but it cannot be denied that the ensuing management shakeup has proved beneficial for tenants. However, greatly increased rents are likely to flow from more recent legislation in the Housing and Local Government Act 1989 relating to the operation of the Housing Revenue Account and new rules for the use of capital receipts. This may lead to tenants viewing the situation differently. On the other hand, the bad memories of being a private tenant are very strong in the generation who experienced the moves from the pre-Second World War slums, and their views will help to inform the present tenant-association activists who are examining the deals on offer. It remains to be seen how far these legislative changes can be effected in practice. If the present government gains another period of office then privatization of the housing services will continue. If an alternative government wins it is hoped that major changes of a different nature will take place, reinstating municipal building as a major avenue of provision, adjusting tax relief and improving benefits to name but a few possibilities.

1.2.5 Status

As a result of all these changes, the chance to unify the housing service was seized upon. It was a step which had been urged by advisory bodies like CHAC for many years. The Institute of Housing tried to establish its professional credentials by promoting the idea of a comprehensive housing service. The idea built on reports by CHAC, Bains and Seebohm, and was designed to help senior housing officers argue for increased status at the time of restructuring. However, the result was patchy with some housing officers becoming heads of comprehensive departments, whilst others remained in fragmented ones, or were absorbed into others.

It also became apparant at the time of re-organization that the housing profession was grossly under-trained. The meagre training available had been given by two separate organizations, the Society of Women Housing Managers and the Institute of Housing (IOH). In 1965 the two professional societies merged and the new body began to promote the housing profession. The Institute has made a further determined effort to professionalize housing by revising its examination syllabi and expanding its educational and training role. This effort has received some backing from the Department of the Environment. However, the multidisciplinary nature of housing makes it difficult to gain recognition as a profession in quite the same way as a lawyer or an engineer.

The Institute, until recently, aimed most of its work at local authorities and their staff, leaving the housing associations to be served by the NFHA. Individual associations became members of the latter body which exists primarily to advise on professional practice. With the blurring of boundaries in housing the two professional bodies are beginning to work together and have some influence on political attitudes to housing, professional practice and the training and education of housing staff.

1.3 Management initiatives

As financial and government pressures increased, specific management and structural initiatives to capitalize on them have risen and declined in popularity. Some of the most popular will now be discussed, first those initiatives relating to organizations as a whole, and second those special initiatives targeted at groups of properties.

1.3.1 Organizations as a whole

Corporate planning

The influence of the corporate planning (CP) idea was mentioned in the first section of this chapter when discussing the re-organization of local government. At its simplest it is a term used to imply that a local authority should plan its future activities as a whole and in a coherent manner. A useful article has been written by Clapham outlining the different meanings of CP, how its practice changed over time as well as the reason for it being introduced. 'The early approach emphasised organisational structures such as chief executives, policy committees, management boards, large directorates instead of many small departments, planning units usually reporting directly to the chief executive' (Clapham, 1985). A book of readings by Greenwood and Stewart (1974) give a further insight to this approach. Later in his article, Clapham suggests that the emphasis switched to decentralized organizational structures. This means that CP will be achieved by 'less formal, ad hoc working groups of officers and members constituted in response to particular issues and disbanded when the work was complete' (Clapham, 1985). Stewart (1971), Hambleton (1978), and Cole and Windle (1990, in print) discuss this approach. The Audit Commission (1985) has also published advice, and argue that local authorities need to develop certain characteristics such as clarity of values and purpose, simple structures, co-ordination through teamwork and delegation and autonomy to allow staff to be closer to the customer; in essence decentralized structures with a sensitive and effective central control. But the Commission (1985) recognizes that 'the strategic approach to planning is dependent on the local situation'. The following three examples of CP from the Audit Commission document demonstrate how different the process may be.

1. Havering   The council produces a three year corporate plan for each service which is reviewed annually. Plans for years two and three are carried out if resources are available. The annual budget is used to monitor the plan.
2. Wrekin DC   This council produced a strategy for the 1980s based on research and statistical analysis into the quality of life and unemployment in the area. Priority client groups were identified and the strategy based on the effect of the recession on the groups.
3. Clwyd Country Council   The council ranks its activities into three priority bands. Expenditure levels are set for each committee and annual reports describe cost activities, identifies shortfalls and possible options.

These examples of current practices suggest that there is an effort to implement the process of corporate planning rather than just the structure, as Clapham argued. Evidence is not available as to how many councils operate a form of CP but the Commission suggests that many do. As a service department at both District and Metropolitan level Housing is a major spender and should have considerable input into the corporate plan. Hence to have the housing functions split between departments reduces the coherence and effectiveness of such input. As a technique CP is useful but is highly dependent for its success on political and professional will and skill.

Decentralization

Decentralization seems to be the current fashion in organizational change. Chapter 2 makes general comments on organizational theory, forms, and decentralization.

Housing associations

In the housing association field, certain organizational ploys have become popular to achieve continuing development. The innovations tend to be confined to the bigger organizations in the inner cities or the regionally based associations.

The first device came about because of the pressure of financial restrictions. Charitable associations set up separate companies, commonly known as 'satellites', which enabled them to borrow on the open market and continue developing. Some associations covenanted profits back to the charity. This idea was picked up by local authorities but was frustrated by central government's regulations. Wholesale transfer of tenants homes to a local authority association is a variation on this initiative.

Similarly, financial pressures pushed associations to consider expanding into different parts of the country, often working through partnerships with local authorities. These associations then take on the face of national organizations, with regional offices and an appropriate decentralized structure. Regional offices act as area bases for housing management and development functions, referring to the centre for policy approvals and financing. Local offices are established for specific projects or small collections of properties. The Glasgow University research (1989) found that these organizations were not regarded as highly as locally based associations, which suggests that they equate to decentralization of a large authority with area offices controlling 6000 plus properties.

A growing form of organization is the consortium of associations, whereby an association with a strong asset base teams up with smaller ones to co-operate on schemes and bid for land. The assets of the combined group can then be used to borrow money. Mergers between associations have already taken place to meet the new requirements of a competitive market and there is a danger that a consortium may have a built-in pressure to this end. It is a matter of opinion whether or not this is good for the voluntary movement of housing associations.

Local authority housing associations

Some local authorities have set up special housing associations to which they have transferred the whole or bulk of their tenants' homes. The intention is to circumvent the Housing Act 1988 which allows tenants to swap to other landlords. Control is retained through councillor and tenant representatives, and the duty to house the homeless has been partially resolved by nomination deals with the association. The primary advantage of a separate association is the access to unrestricted borrowing on the open market which enables renovation and building of new homes to continue. The main disadvantages are funding the transfer of properties and deciding rent levels. These factors are crucial to the future viability of such associations. Newbury DC has transferred 7000 homes to the newly formed West Berkshire Housing Association with the tenants' consent. Its committee includes tenant representatives and councillors. The council's housing department was also transferred, with the exception of the homeless person's unit and housing strategy section (Inside Housing 8.12.89). Chiltern DC and Sevenoaks DC have carried out similar voluntary transfers. Other proposed transfers of tenants have not been successful. In Redbridge, London, tenants rejected a transfer proposal as have those in two Essex authorities. It is early days to judge whether the associations will be able to keep their promises to maintain rents at a reasonable level, carry out the improvements etc. and continue giving tenants a good service. An additional problem may be that transferred authority staff will find it difficult to adjust to the ethos of the voluntary movement.

As a variation on the transfer dodges, some authorities have considered formally transferring the management (not the ownership) of their housing service to a private management company or an existing housing association (Inside Housing 19.1.90). It is probable that the organization of a management company would be similar to that of a housing association, but the question must be asked, who will set the policies on rent and arrears, and what will happen about improvements and major repairs? This may be answered at Rochester and Medway where tenants voted for a transfer to a non-profit making private company registered with the Registrar of Friendly Societies (Inside Housing 18.5.90 and 8.6.90). Guarantees on rent levels are built into the constitution and a majority of three-quarters of the tenants is required to change it. The Management Board comprises four salaried chief officers of the Council, three outside Directors, two tenants and an elected member of staff. Tenant representation is rather low.

Transfer of properties to Trusts

As part of the government's radical policies for council housing the Housing Act 1988 introduced the idea of Housing Action Trusts (HATs). These Trusts were to be set up to tackle the concentrations of rundown council housing by temporarily taking over homes in designated local authority areas, in order to carry out physical improvements quickly and efficiently. The Trusts would be run by Boards, the members being appointed by the Secretary of State, and include representatives of the tenants and the local authorities. Tenants want be given a chance to vote on whether a Trust should be established. If a majority were against the idea the order designating the area would not be pursued. If agreed then tenants would become, temporarily tenants of the Trust enjoying exactly the same rights as secure tenants. Once the Trust had completed its work, tenants could make a choice about their future landlord either exercising the right to buy, returning to the local authority or choosing one of the 'tenant choice' schemes. Alternatively they could set up a management or tenant co-operative, estate management board or a local housing association. Six HATs were proposed, but all bit the dust. Either consultants' reports were adverse or ballots of tenants views resulted in their rejection. The anti-vote seemed to express an anxiety about who a future landlord might be, with particular fears about returning to private landlordism. However, in 1991 Kingston upon Hull Council proposed a HAT in their area and convinced tenants of its value. The DOE seems to have altered its views in relation to local influence and has give guarantees about rent levels, rights to return to the Council and making money available to buy back properties. A second HAT has been agreed by the tenants of Waltham Forest Council.

The heralds of the HAT initiative were the Stocksbridge Village Trust and Thamesmead Town Ltd, neither of which have fulfilled the government's hopes for a new type of entrepreneurial organization. Both organizations have run into financial difficulties and as a consequence have had to raise rents and reduce their targets for refurbishment and new building. The freedom of an appointed board to make immediate decisions has not led to a markedly more successful way of managing rundown estates than an elected council.

1.4 Special initiatives

In an attempt to overcome the management problems of unpopular estates owned by the local authorities a number of special initiatives directed to local management have been introduced. The umbrella for these initiatives started as the Urban Housing Renewal Unit of the DOE in 1985 and then changed its name to Estate Action. The main thrust has been towards tenant involvement, specialist advice and information, offering additional borrowing approvals to the councils concerned and Urban Programme grants where appropriate. Authorities have been asked to submit schemes for improving rundown estates by using either their own resources, Priority Estate Project (PEP) teams, or the Community Refurbishment Scheme (CRS). Some have been relatively successful but all have the problem of what happens after the special monies cease. Few of the local authorities have the resources to maintain the level of spending and there is a danger of estates lapsing into decay for a second time with the subsequent disillusion of tenants. The two most important initiatives, PEPs and CRS are further discussed, with a comment on management co-operatives.

1.4.1 Priority estates project

The ideas of the PEP experiment are rooted in the past. Octavia Hill's intensive but authoritarian management methods of the 19th century (Darley, 1989) have been slightly turned to involve tenants in decision making and produce a locally based and locally controlled management. By 1979, there were considerable worries about the unpopularity of many council estates. A pilot scheme funded by the DOE involving tenants and estate staff was launched with three local authorities, Bolton, Hackney and Lambeth. 'The basic idea was not new or difficult: to establish a local management office, to carry out meticulously the landlord's responsibility for rent, repairs, letting property and maintaining the environment of the estate; and to give tenants a chance to exercise maximum control over their homes and neighbourhood.' (Power, 1984). The results of the pilot scheme encouraged the DOE to persuade other local authorities to take up the initiative. In 1982 the PEP surveyed a number of authorities who had problems with unpopular estates, and selected 20 estates to examine in greater depth.

The conclusions drawn from the survey, suggested the need for estate-based management and permanent local offices (Power, 1984). These conclusions must be regarded critically. Two Housing Centre Seminars were devoted to the subject (Housing Review 1984 and 1985) where worries were expressed about the long term outcome of the projects, the diversion of resources from other council estates and insufficient staff training. Only a limited amount of money is available from central government via the Estate Action Budget or Urban Programme. However, the expectation is that an estate budget will be created and day-to-day management be paid for out of the Housing Revenue Account (HRA). The Housing Act 1989 s.76 stipulates that there is a duty to prevent a debit balance in the HRA so that there will often be a danger of financial cuts in some authorities to achieve this target.

A useful guide to such locally based housing management has been produced by Power (1987). A typical local organization is shown in Figure 1.1.

The establishment of local offices will in many cases be tied in with decentralization policies, but it is of advantage for an estate to be designated a PEP to gain extra resources. A further survey of PEP schemes in nine authorities in England and Wales found that 'because the local team delivers the service direct, the whole operation is simplified, accelerated and accountable to tenants' (Power, 1987). In general, PEP local offices cost marginally more to run than a central organization but this is offset by savings, for example, in increased lettings and cleaning of estates. The PEP offers advice on implementation of locally based management.

As a structure for delivering services there is no doubt that local offices can be effective, tenants have quick access to staff and repairs etc. can be completed rapidly by local teams. Successful projects may lead to organizational change throughout a housing department and there is evidence to suggest that the general move to decentralization of services has been fuelled by the PEP research.

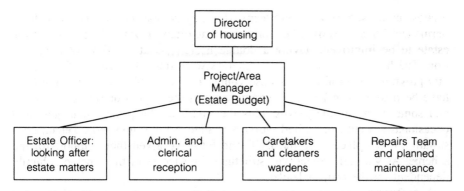

Figure 1.1 Organization of a local office.
Source: Adapted from the PEP Guide to Local management, No. 1, PEP Estate Action, DOE, Welsh Office, 1987.

1.4.2 Management co-operatives (co-ops)

This form of organization is in reality locally based management by the tenants. The basic principle is that the members of the co-ops, who are the tenants themselves, become responsible for the management and maintenance of their homes and the estate. Essentially the co-op acts as an agent to carry out all the landlord's statutory responsibilities. This form of organization gives tenants control over the factors which most frustrate them, that is the repairs service, the external environment and influencing who their neighbours are. There are variations between co-ops according to the background of the tenants involved, the degree of delegation by the landlord and the finance available. Research for the DOE (Matthews, 1981; Downey, Matthews and Mason, 1982) based on local authority co-ops suggested that successful co-ops were dependent on the motivation and selection of the tenant group, the support they received from the authority and the timing of the handover of responsibility. A national study of all types of co-operative housing in McCafferty and Riley (1989) revealed that only 20% were under tenant management, with landlords being both council and housing associations. It is clear that this type of organization appeals to a small number of tenants. There is a further discussion of co-ops in Chapter 6.

1.4.3 Community refurbishment schemes (CRS)

The aim of these schemes was to utilize local people as a resource to improve their environment and carry out minor home repairs. The CRS used unemployed people to undertake work programmes on rundown council estates supervised by a project team who may or may not be seconded from permanent housing staff. The workforce was often drawn from tenants of the estate to be improved, having a double usefulness at the time of consultation. The labour costs of the first schemes were funded by the MSC community programme but after its demise youngsters on Employment Training (ET) have been used. The Urban Programme funds the capital outlay for an office and some of its running costs, plus the salary of the project managers and occasionally a core of skilled workers (Estate Action, undated). Tenant consultation takes place once the DOE and ET have given their support for the scheme. As with all project type structures the success of the scheme is highly dependent on the project leader.

A programme of this nature will not necessarily solve the problems of a rundown estate and should be seen only as the first stage of a commitment to locally-based management. The success of the pioneer schemes on Merseyside led to the extension of the work to the rest of England. A good example of such a scheme is the Orchard Estate in Hull. However, there is a move by the DOE to use the Estate Action Budget to encourage environmental improvement by other means, so the long term future of CRS is uncertain.

1.5 Additional techniques to assist change

The process of change in housing is causing a great deal of pain. The resource base has been reduced in financial and people terms, the housing stock is deteriorating and a proportion of tenants are disatisfied. Organizations must alter to cope with the new demands and at the same time take account of their staff resources and interests. Most people feel threatened by change so that, for example, re-structuring plans which seem rational to senior staff are seen by the rank and file as a danger. However, there is greater danger in not changing to meet the new challenges. The IOH (1987) suggests that 'people who work in Housing Departments and Housing Associations probably have more to gain than to fear from the structural changes in managing and providing social housing. . .'. Increasingly, courses are being run to suggest ways and means by which change can be accomplished successfully. They include ways of training, developing and appraising staff performance, involving tenants, measuring the performance of the organization and the application of computer technology. It is these techniques which will be discussed briefly.

1.5.1 Staff performance

Increasing pressure is being put on housing organizations to ensure that their future staffing plans incorporate training, development and appraisal of the workforce. The management literature published by the Audit Commission and the Local Government Training Board (LGTB) tends to promote the use of a variation on 'management by objectives' (MBO), as one approach to planning, organizing and executing work. MBO is a system which has been described as 'a style or system of management which attempts to relate or-gan-izational goals to individual performance and development through the involve-ment of all levels of management' (Mullins 1985). The basis of the system is:

- the setting of targets and objectives for the organization;
- participation by individual managers in agreeing unit objectives and criteria of performance;
- review and appraisal of results.

Drucker (1968), Odiorne (1965) and Humble (1972) are writers who developed and popularized the system, which is used in both public and private sectors.

Such a system asks staff to set their own goals in relation to a given task rather than be told what to do. Measurement of performance then relates to the outcome of the task rather than the ability of an individual to follow orders. As most housing organizations run on sets of procedures, apart from setting general policies, this means a radical change in working patterns. It is a satisfying method of working as it allows staff to make a personal contribution and to achieve a greater degree of participation and responsibility. The reverse side of the coin is that it may place too great an emphasis on individual job definitions and management structure and assume no conflict between private and organizational goals.

The more participative approach would seem to be an appropriate model when managing change as it takes staff into the confidence of management and tries to take them along with the change. Mullins (1985) suggests that certain principles must be applied which include a priority 'to create an environment of trust and shared commitment, and to involve staff in decisions and actions which affect them'. As part of creating this environment both local authorities and housing associations are sending staff, particularly middle management, to attend 'staff development' courses which allow people to identify their needs within the overall strategies of their organizations. This follows the Audit Commission (1986) suggestions that there should be concentration on 'improving the quality of middle management, by investing in more and better training'. The philosophy of this type of management embraces all staff so that frontline and senior staff will also receive appropriate training.

1.5.2 Tenant involvement

The rise of participation has led to tenant involvement being used as a technique of management. Since 1980, tenants have been given rights to consultation on housing management matters and this was extended by the Housing and Planning Act 1986 to consultation before disposal of estates to other landlords. The Housing Act 1988, after a struggle, provides for tenants' ballots if a change of landlord is proposed. These rights have fuelled a move towards involvement of tenants in running their own homes. The PEP and Tenant TPAS have also been influential in spreading a change in attitude on the part of landlords to tenant involvement.

Cynics may see it as a means to placate tenants or to offload costs and management in such initiatives as tenants' co-ops. Most organizations formally committed to tenant involvement like TPAS, National Consumer Council, and the national tenant organizations hold the view that asking the users of the service what is needed is a necessary contribution to sensible housing policies. Where tenants have had the chance to participate as advisors on design or drawing up new tenancy agreements their contributions have been valuable (Ash 1982). Certainly their voices have been heard in the matter of ballots on moving from a local authority to another landlord. In terms of change tenants may be seen as a resource taking a positive interest in their surroundings and, through co-operation, cutting the cost of management whilst improving their own living standards. Participation is the theme of Chapter 6 and will be pursued in more detail there.

1.5.3 Performance indicators

The introduction of 'performance indicators' as a measure of the success of local authorities and housing associations is a manifestation of how the tools of business management are being transplanted to the public domain. It is, however, a very useful tool. There is a great paucity of data on performance and costs for social housing providers, even though landlords and tenants have a vested interest in monitoring the delivery of the housing service (Glasgow University, 1989). In the past, monitoring the budget and tenant satisfaction surveys have been ways of doing this, but are limited in application. There have been attempts to develop indicators, initially by the Audit Commission (1985, 1986). Crude indicators such as numbers of vacant homes (voids), amount of rent collected, arrears recovery as a proportion of gross debit and staffing levels give a measure of performance. There was criticism of the findings by Glasgow University, 1989, but the government has decided to use indicators as a measuring stick for itself and tenants. The Local Government and Housing Act 1989 s.167 (1) make reports to tenants on housing functions mandatory, using performance indicators as the basis of the reports. (DOE Circular 19/90).

The IOH in its (unpublished) reply to a consultation paper on performance indicators in 1989 (DOE 1989) questioned the use of some of the indicators in the form proposed. For example, the indicators on housing lettings reflected the size and nature of the allocations task rather than performance. Tenants are more interested in the length of time it takes to process an application, make a home visit and receive an offer of housing. The information will, however, be a starting point to ask questions, although tenants will need education and guidance to understand the complexities of their local housing administration. The IOH has also combined with TPAS to produce indicators for measuring tenant participation (IOH/TPAS, 1989).

The voluntary sector introduced the idea of indicators in Standards for Housing Management (NFHA, 1987). This was followed by the Housing Corporation's publication Performance Expectations (1989), a document for staff and management committees covering all aspects of housing management, to be used as a monitoring guide by the Housing Corporation. Changes were also proposed concerning performance indicators in the statistical return HAR10/1. Information on these specific indicators must be submitted to the Corporation and be available for tenants. The indicators, like those demanded from the local authorities are basic management facts rather than sophisticated measurements of performance.

The resource implications, for housing organizations, of complying with central government's demand for data and informing tenants is considerable. There is no denying that assessment of performance is crucial to improving the housing service. However, the expense in time and resources may not give a sufficient pay off in terms of tenants' involvement or enhanced management standards, which are the primary objectives. In efforts to meet performance targets there may be a danger of discriminating against groups who do not have a strong bargaining position. For example in meeting a target to fill empty tenancies people may be forced into accepting unsuitable housing and others overlooked. The need for efficiency is fulfilled, but at the expense of tenants and applicants. Setting effective indicators and evaluating results could become a new housing industry!

1.5.4 Information technology

Computer technology is a means by which greater efficiency, quicker communication and more flexible ways of organizing can be achieved. An IOH Computer Working Party (1984) surveyed local authorities and housing associations in England and Wales, and found that the use of computers tended to be restricted to repetitive financial work and some estate management functions. Further surveys of associations by Goodrich (1986) and Lewis (1989) show a similar picture, although there is evidence of a greater use of database packages and spreadsheets. A new study is underway at Salford University to investigate the existing use of information technology by housing agencies in England and Wales. Such a study will disseminate information on the range of options open to organizations. The improved ability of computers to talk to one another has enhanced the efficiency of decentralized organizations and in some cases made decentralization possible, as is argued in Chapter 2. For example, a national association can be networked to its regions, thus being able to store common information which can be tapped into, as well as monitor and control financial functions. Alternatively, micro-computers allow staff in small offices to set up their own systems and create local cost centres. The use of micros and multi-user systems gives flexibility to organizations but the updating of such hardware can be expensive. In a fast developing field the problem of what to buy is a headache.

The most common functions that are computerized are rent collection and accounting, benefits, mortgages, sales, maintenance and repair, waiting lists and allocations, grants office systems, and information on properties. Computerization has not reduced staff but has made it possible to have quicker access to information and store it in a smaller space. It has become easier to monitor functions, produce reports and forecast trends. With the introduction of legislation to keep tenants informed it will be doubly important to produce information quickly and in an easily understandable form. The introduction of computing has often given an organization the chance to review its procedures and assess the value of information held.

A growing use of computers is in the area of financial planning and modelling (Tong, Wilson and Ellis 1986). Many housing schemes use private sector money and it is standard practice in the financial world for business plans and financial risks to be analysed. Managers will require new skills in financial analysis and costings and new software packages are available to help. The most commonly used is the spreadsheet which enables the user to enter and manipulate figures in a calculation to explore a series of options (Stanford, 1989). Associations are also developing financial models to project the likely costs of new-build and rehabilitation schemes. Assumptions and variables are built in and can be manipulated. One particular use of this technique in 'Risk Analysis' is now a part of financial planning in the joint operations of public and private partners.

Conclusions

This overview of housing organizations has looked briefly at the reasons for change in the last two decades, special management initiatives and those involving whole organizations, and finally techniques to manage change. The past 20 years have seen considerable organizational change in both local authorities and housing associations. External pressures such as political ideology and government reports, social change, and the rise of participation have been suggested as major reasons for the change. Internal pressures have been the result of organizations expanding and changing to meet new roles and needs. The housing profession has also changed and expanded and is seeking a leading role in the field. Management fashions come and go, often introduced as an academic idea which gets taken up and is finally dropped or modified in some way. 'Corporate planning', in the guise of 'Management by Objectives' is an example of this, and is enjoying a revival. Currently, 'decentralization' holds the stage with management hoping that it will prove a more humane and local service for tenants.

Linked to the need to ensure that poor estates are improved, some authorities are exploring the idea of transferring ownership of homes to local authority housing associations. This will enable the new organization to avoid public sector spending restrictions. Conversely, central government is trying to set up Housing Action Trusts which will designate rundown authority estates as eligible for special funding and eventual diversity of ownership.

Other initiatives such as the Priority Estates Projects and Management Co-ops try to ensure that tenants have a say in their affairs. Tenant involvement is also being used as a technique for management by landlords. To help this process and improve management generally, performance indicators have been introduced. At the moment many are crude but with the help of computer technology a high level of sophistication may be achieved. Both authorities and associations are increasing their computer capacity and are finding that the technology gives greater flexibility of organization. Finally the staff who are a prime resource are demanding proper training to meet the challenge of modern housing management.

2

Decentralization

2.1 Introduction

Decentralization has been a major trend in organizational change within the housing field over the past ten years. It has affected organizations of widely varying structure and size. Chapter 2 summarizes initially the general influences moulding organizational structures and examines their operation in a number of case studies of decentralization. Finally a range of potential conflicts that may be generated by decentralization are identified and used to illustrate specific aspects of organizational design.

Any organization, regardless of size or purpose, must perform certain tasks in order to achieve its overall objectives. These primary tasks in turn require the execution of numerous subsidiary, detailed tasks. The structure of an organization provides a framework within which all these operations can be efficiently and effectively completed; a reference point for workers in relation to their peers and the means by which both employees and customers understand the organization and are enabled to use its services.

However, to achieve optimum efficiency no organization can rely on good structure alone. The importance of expertise, co-operation and motivation within the workforce must be recognized.

The major influences on type of organizational structure can be identified as follows (Handy, 1985).

1. Size   Local Government units for instance can range from Birmingham (population 998 000; housing stock 121 006) to Teesdale (population 24 900; housing stock 1776) (Other housing organizations can be equally variable Municipal Year Book, 1989.)
2. History and origins   Local Government for example must accommodate a dual decision-making process, both administrative and political, and has a history of bureaucratic structure.

3. Available technology   As developments in Information Technology (IT) provide wider and faster access to basic information organizations are both stimulated and enabled to change their structure and method of operation.
4. Human relations   Organizations are established and maintained by individuals whose interaction will influence decision making as well as the nature and direction of organizational development.
5. External environment   Organizations do not exist in a policy vacuum, and Local Authority structures in particular must bend to political and social pressures which are external to them and their objectives. This was increasingly apparant in housing during the Thatcher years.
6. Organizational rationale   Structures may also reflect aims seemingly unconnected with their primary objectives. Local Housing Authorities embrace notions of equity, social welfare and democratic control in addition to their primary role as enablers and providers of housing.

These issues provide a framework within which to assess the influence of decentralization on the changing structure of housing organizations.

2.2 Changing face of public sector housing

In the twentieth century the provision of rented housing has been through a gradual revolution. From the monopoly position held by the private landlord we are now in a situation where the majority (73%) of rented housing is provided and managed by local authorities (Central Statistical Office, 1988). Such large scale public landlordism has not been achieved without problems or criticism. Notable failings — such as the extensive mass building system and high rise construction during the 1960s and 1970s — under investment from the 1970s onwards, coupled with poor management, have all contributed to a public sector housing 'crisis'. Now, at a time of record homelessness and evident housing need, public landlords have only a deteriorating, dwindling stock in which they are restricted from investing. Faced with this crisis the tenor of Government policy has mirrored other aspects of its economic and social policy — removing 'burdens' on the public purse, introducing 'choice' and emphasizing individual responsibility for housing conditions. To achieve these objectives it has sought to change the balance between housing tenures and between those organizations providing rented housing. After a period of increasing bitterness and antagonism between central and local government about the extent of control, levels of spending and priorities in service provision, the 1987 White Paper (Cmnd. 214) argued for a reducing role for local authority provision and an increase in the role of the private and 'independent' rented sector. To date the effect has been an increase in owner occupation at the expense of the public rented sector rather than revitalization of the private rented market. While meeting some governmental objectives, this has done little to alleviate the legacy of problems facing local authority housing departments.

However, these have not been the only recent changes occurring in housing. Change has also been evident within the local authority housing sector. New organizational structures have been devised, management practices have been reviewed, decision making structures opened up and a different culture adopted. For many authorities these changes culminated in a radical move in housing departments — to decentralization.

This wave of interest in decentralization originated with the decision in 1980 by Walsall Metropolitan Council to establish 32 neighbourhood housing offices across the borough. The radical and ambitious plan replaced the existing central hierarchy with a significantly flattened, dispersed structure. With this as a blueprint other (predominantly Labour controlled) urban authorities — for example Islington, Lambeth, Hackney, Manchester — set out with similar intentions but with more varied long-term success (Hambleton and Hoggett, 1984; London Borough of Islington, 1987; Powell, 1981; Seex, 1987).

These early decentralization initiatives are all characterized by their origins in the attempted revitalization of municipal socialism in the face of a hostile and confident Conservative government. Politically inspired decentralization was seen as a means of regenerating the power base of Labour councils through empowering local communities and breaking down some of the older, discredited, paternalistic and bureaucratic structures. By improving local services, making locally based decisions with rather than for people, it was hoped they would support and protect local councils against the threat of increasing central control by the government (Blunkett and Green, 1983; Seabrook, 1984; Boddy and Fudge, 1984).

2.3 Why decentralization?

It is easier to see what decentralization was a reaction against rather than what it was a move towards. Terms such as impersonal, remote, uncaring, too large, unco-operative, 'buck' passing, have all been used to describe local authority housing organizations. Alienated tenants, frustrated staff and ineffective councillors felt constrained by the rigid structures, outmoded specialisms and paternalism existing in housing management. Users, providers and outside commentators alike agreed that the structure, management and service to the tenant and ratepayer left much to be desired (Audit Commission, 1986; Institute of Housing, 1987; NFHA, 1985b).

Earlier in this chapter we indicated that the determinants of organizational structure suggested the bureaucratic model as the most appropriate for the provision of local authority services. Classic bureaucracies are characterized by a hierarchy of authority, specialist functional divisions and a system of rules and procedures to ensure impartiality in decisions. Stewart argues that many of the criticisms levelled at local housing departments are in fact criticisms of classic bureaucracies and should not be accepted without a deeper understanding of the nature of organizational development (Stewart in Hambleton and Hoggett, 1984). Bureaucracy has been the accepted model for local authority services because it meets the needs of the organizational rationale.

> In the case of public sector organisations in particular there is a demand for uniformity of treatment, regularity of procedures and accountability for their operations. This leads to adherence to specified rules and procedures which limit the degree of discretion exercised by management, and to the keeping of detailed records. (Mullins, 1985)

The critique of local authority service provision which has prompted the move to decentralization has focused on the very foundations of bureaucratic structure. The role of regulation and procedures necessary for the correct and fair distribution of resources has become corrupted so that regulations are seen as an end in themselves, a barrier to responsiveness rather than an aid to fairness. Specialist expertise becomes associated with official status and is seen as a means of protecting power bases by limiting access to knowledge. Structures and hierarchies become a means to avoid making decisions rather than a framework for accountability.

Given such an analysis of the failings of local authority services the alternative offered by decentralization was eagerly adopted. It was viewed as an antidote to the excesses of the large organizations managing council housing after 1974. It provided both an administrative critique of the deficiencies in the organization and delivery of housing services and a political vision of community involvement and regeneration.

Decentralization resulted in a move away from the traditionally specialized, hierarchical, large and impersonal departments of the past. The changes have provided new forms of organization. But it is not without its own problems. Organizations concerned with the distribution of scarce public resources within a framework of local democracy must still have some rational, impartial means of performing their functions.

Decentralization is clearly not simply a passing fad. Too many authorities have now adopted the philosophy, entirely or in part. It has become central to current developments in the management of rented housing. Decentralized services have been the focus for considerable investigation as attempts have been made to evaluate the impact of organizational change on the provision of public housing services.

2.4 The experience of decentralization

Research* examining the form and extent of decentralization amongst housing authorities in the north of England has provided some insight to the way
in which many organizations have adapted the philosophy of decentralization to their own requirements. In the 'second wave' of decentralizing authorities the aims and objectives have been examined, showing how the earlier
politically motivated plans had been moulded and modified into mana-
gerially orientated proposals, enabling the continued existence of reformed
bureaucracies.

The specific purpose of the research was to examine the nature and extent
of decentralization amongst housing authorities in the north of England as
much of the previous work had concentrated on the earlier initiatives in Walsall
and the South East. Little work had been done on the extent to which the
ideas had been adopted by northern authorities and whether they had similar
aims and objectives.

The impact of decentralization amongst housing authorities has clearly been
felt right across the region. As a description of organizational structure it has
been widely adopted. Thirty five larger authorities (more than 6000 stock)
had implemented decentralization plans since 1980 and a further eight were
preparing to do so. This represents a majority of all larger housing authorities in the north.

The degree to which the term decentralization has been applied to restruc-
tured organizations warrants its deeper investigation within the wider context
of understanding organizational development and design. Decentralization is
often viewed as a reaction against the failings of bureaucracies, but with
imprecise such objectives the idea can be adapted to meet many, diverse
ends. Decentralization can be all things to all people. In the absence of clearly
defined and agreed goals, the decentralization of an organization can result
in the failure to achieve any advance or satisfaction. Managers, politicians and
consumers may all criticize the existing structure and operation and advocate
'decentralization' as the appropriate solution but without the precise definition

---

* The research carried out in 1988 was undertaken in two phases. First, a regional
survey involved distributing four questionnaires to each local authority (116). These
were directed to different 'actors' — Chief Housing Officers, Chief Executives, Council
Leaders and the Chairperson of the Housing Committee — to provide differing perspectives on the process of decentralization. A full discussion of the survey results
can be found in a series of working papers produced by the Research Team (Windle,
Cole and Arnold, 1988).

The second phase of the research involved a series of four case studies in which
particular authorities were the focus for more detailed analysis around particular themes.

of objectives such as 'local accountability', 'responsiveness' or 'accessibility' conflicts between the interests of different groups will arise.

Although nearly all these initiatives had taken place in Labour controlled councils, they appeared to differ in their approach from the earlier radical attempts at revitalizing local socialism. The vast majority (69%) had been promoted by housing officers who, having recognized the criticisms directed at housing management, looked to decentralization to solve some of their problems. Problems and inadequacies identified in terms of bureaucratic blockages to good services seemed to suggest a resolution in terms of organizational restructuring. The need to improve services and provide them in an accessible and responsive manner were the primary objectives of the majority of decentralizing authorities.

In the survey Chief Housing Officers were asked to rank a series of objectives on their decentralization. The majority emphasized what Paul Hoggett has termed 'consumerist' aspects (Hambleton and Hoggett, 1987), highlighting service delivery, responsiveness and public relations, rather than the 'collectivist' model emphasizing service democracy (Windle, Arnold and Cole, 1988a).

That managers have predominantly managerial objectives is not surprising. However, a parallel survey of Housing Committee Chairs illustrates similar objectives amongst local politicians. Direct comparisons here are not legitimate because of differences in rates of response to both surveys, but increased service responsiveness was clearly also the primary political motivation for new organizational structures (Cole, Arnold and Windle, 1988a).

In some cases, decentralization has been adopted as a strategy for wholesale departmental restructuring, involving rationalization of responsibilities, enhanced training, extensive recruitment and professionalization. The 'Walsall model' used the strategy to change the dominant organizational culture. The more prevalent scenario, however, among the survey authorities involved more modest, pragmatic objectives, the result of incremental drift rather than politically inspired, comprehensive forward strategy.

An additional influence on the extent of decentralization in the north clearly originated from powerful external sources. Over half indicated that their proposals had included Priority Estate Projects or Estate Action Projects. Thus the effect on structural change brought about in local government through the economic controls of central government cannot be underestimated.

Earlier it was noted that a framework is needed within which integral parts of an organization can inter-relate. Where one component undergoes a process of internal reorganization then its relationship to other components will also be affected. Yet nearly 60% of our respondents had involved only the narrowly defined responsibilities of the housing department. Changing the structure and function of other service departments was not a priority. This is a salient issue for those concerned with organizational design and change.

Can the reorganization of one part of a complex whole be effective if other related sections do not recognize it and accommodate themselves to the change?

As an antidote to bureaucracy decentralization has been associated with simplified hierarchies; a broad based pyramid in which the front line, neighbourhood service is strengthened at the expense of the remote, central, back line support. Yet few of the decentralized authorities in the survey had actually adopted the flatter organizational structure implied by the decentralization philosophy. The majority employed instead a multi-tiered approach, apparently grafting additional local service points on to existing networks rather than undertaking a process of wholesale organizational restructuring. This probably reflects the incremental nature of many of the schemes in the north in contrast to some of the earlier more radical initiatives. The piecemeal approach has advantages over the 'big bang' method since, even in the latter, time is required in order for new relationships and networks to be established, new skills developed and staff assimilated. Yet there is a danger in incremental change that the momentum and commitment to a fundamental change in organizational culture will be dissipated as traditional bureaucratic practices seek to reassert themselves.

The degree to which local authority housing departments have associated themselves with the objectives of decentralized service provision is not disputed. The practices are now part of the mainstream in service delivery. What is less clear is the extent to which these often traumatic upheavals have changed fundamentally the actual process of service delivery. Structures have been reorganized, but what effect has this had on those who provide the service and the quality and cost of that service?

Peripheral or superficial changes are more usual than successful fundamental change as a result of decentralization. However, other features of bureaucracy — the technical specialist and the compartmentalism of knowledge — have been challenged by most decentralizing organizations. Eighty three percent cited an increase in generic working practices occurred as a result of reorganization. This change in working practices has far reaching implications for workers, trades unions and managers. Changing traditional attitudes to long standing working methods, developing new skills and retraining staff are issues which virtually all authorities implementing decentralization have had to face.

The objective given highest priority by most authorities was 'improving service delivery'. This clearly implies some form of evaluation and measurement criteria which when defined further highlight the diversity of perspectives on evaluation and quality measurement. Improvement of services for managers is invariably translated as lower arrears or void levels. Improved service for consumers may mean the opportunity to discuss a problem in privacy with a sympathetic and knowledgeable housing officer. Measurement of the former is easier than the latter, but both are important in an assessment of the effect of decentralization.

The survey could only begin to assess the way in which managers felt decentralization had affected their organization. Improvements were in fact identified by the majority in the management of voids and decreased letting times. Other management aspects, such as levels of arrears and the average repair time, were thought to have been less universally improved by decentralization, but managers were nevertheless positive about the potential for improvements. Such self-assessment must be interpreted with some caution, as few authorities had (at that time) instigated any formal methods of evaluating service changes and assessment was largely on an intuitive basis. However, there was cautious optimism about the overall success of decentralization. While no respondents considered that all their original objectives had been achieved, 86% felt they had reached at least half their desired aims.

2.4.1   Resources

Improvements in efficiency (or productivity) are brought about by investment in organizational infrastructure. When applied to the public sector, efficiency through decentralization has also required investment and thus increased resources are a feature for most — at least in the short or medium term. The vast majority of respondents quoted increased capital and revenue costs associated with investment in new technology and additional office accommodation essential for effective decentralization. A small minority had achieved some savings in senior, administrative and manual staff costs.

This initial requirement for extra resources has clearly limited or curtailed the potential for decentralization in the survey region. Despite the potential for long-term savings advocated by some proponents of local housing management (Power, 1987a), the initial expense at a time of overall resource constraint for housing authorities has been a limiting influence on the scope and nature of structural change for many authorities.

Decentralization as a form of structural change is not solely concerned with patterns and organization charts. It is also part of a process of altering the way housing services are perceived and delivered. The effect of that change on the different 'actors' involved is also crucial to the ultimate effectiveness of the new organizational structure.

Those working within the reorganized department have had to learn new skills, adapt to different working environments which are often more exposed and isolated, and deal with the consequence of accessibility — that is increased demands. While this can be a stimulating and challenging improvement from a routine, office-bound job, it brings with it new demands and pressures with which many have found it increasingly stressful to cope. Staff must be committed to and understand the wider aims of decentralization if they are to implement these in their daily work, and thus complement structural decentralization with a fundamental change in the way in which services are perceived.

With such high priority accorded to the consumerist aims of decentralization, the level of tenant satisfaction with local services must be a crucial measure of their success. Chief Officers were cautious about the extent to which this had increased — one third honestly reported that they did not know. Our own surveys with consumer groups have indicated strong support for the aims of decentralization — it 'makes sense' to the consumer. However, many tenants are also stern critics of any inadequacies in the service and are usually vociferous in their demands for improvements.

This survey of authorities in the north confirmed the view that a significant change in the organization and structure of housing departments had been occurring in recent years. It also appeared that the earlier examples of decentralization had been adapted to suit the less ambitious predominantly managerial priorities concerned with improving image and service delivery, rather than the overtly political objectives of the 'collectivist' model. Housing managers adopted the philosophy as a means of improving services and responding to criticisms. They then convinced often reluctant politicians of the validity of their proposals and the necessity of additional finance to achieve them.

2.4.2 Summary

The significance of the change has been great. The philosophy of service to the public has been reviewed; presentation of services has been updated; partnership in decision making has been encouraged in place of paternalism. The working conditions and environment of thousands of housing staff have been affected, tenants' expectations have been raised and new demands made on local managers. In some cases, involvement of local politicians and tenants in decisions about spending priorities have developed out of, or alongside, administrative restructuring, changing the relationships between consumers, managers and politicians.

No single view is appropriate to analyse the effect of decentralization or the process through which change is achieved. Similarly, no single structure is appropriate in all circumstances. The constraints and influences on organizational design dictate that structure will evolve to reflect local circumstances and priorities. This process of evolution and change is important in our overall appreciation of decentralization. Analysis of the change illustrates not only how services can be improved but also how any attempt to change the theory and practice of an organization within an essentially unchanged wider structure will generate conflicts of its own.

Decentralization has changed structures, improved services and altered working practices. Attempts have been made to modify bureaucracies criticized for their outdated approach to consumer needs. But this raises many more issues when, as Stewart argues, the need for some form of bureaucratic distribution of resources is still apparent (Stewart in Hambleton and Hoggett, 1984).

Tensions are a feature of all organizations — large or small, simple or complex — as the interaction of processes, individuals and groups gradually alters delicate power balances. The tensions identified in section 2.5 are not all exclusive to decentralized organizations, or to local authorities. However, as decentralization disrupts existing patterns and imposes new relationships, the opportunity for potential conflict arises in a number of situations. Thus, analysis of decentralization exposes the sources of many problems faced by those managing fundamental changes in all organizations.

2.5 Conflict between diversity and uniformity

Decentralization can be viewed as a response to the pressures for diversity (Handy, 1985). It is a recognition of the need to be able to provide ser-vices that meet locally defined priorities. Responding to these, rather than imposing a universal centrally determined response, is a primary purpose of introducing a decentralized system of service provision. Yet this essentially differentiated approach to service delivery is contrary to the whole tradition of local authority structure and organization. 'If the aim is the application of rules, then sensitivity, responsiveness and involvement can undermine the rules' (Stewart in Hambleton and Hoggett, 1984). Achieving the balance between uniformity and diversity should be the basis for discussion and consultation in the initial stages of all proposals to decentralize housing services. There is a need to maintain a fair distribution of resources whilst ensuring that flexibility exists to respond to particular areas of need.

The balance is a delicate one. In some respects decentralization increases the need to be vigilant about uniform standards and procedures. The organization has responsibility for the whole authority and the rules and procedures characteristic of centralized bureaucracies to ensure equity of provision are still relevant in a decentralized structure. However, procedures which do not recognize local variation may have the effect of disadvantaging sections of the community in their access to services.

Fowler summarizes one solution to this dilemma as 'centralisation of policy — decentralisation of practice' (Fowler, 1988). This involves a change in the relationship between the centre and the periphery and a rationalization of their respective roles. Thus the centre becomes a strategic unit responsible for developing and monitoring policies while the application of those policies is the sole responsibility of the local service delivery point.

2.6 Conflict between rationality and responsiveness

The dismantling of excessive bureaucracy must be balanced against the need to maintain rationality of decision making. The allocation of resources must be seen to be fair and impartial while still responding to local needs. Such processes raise the potential for conflict when decisions are apparently subject to partial opinions and lobbying from interested parties. But decentralization also provides the opportunity to overcome such problems and actually improve the decision-making process by utilizing local knowledge and priorities. Rational decisions may be impartial but they may also have little relevance to actual consumer needs. How often have we heard complaints such as, 'they came and fitted the whole estate with central heating, but what we really need is new windows so that all the heat doesn't disappear through the gaps!'? By making an overall fair and rational distribution of resources, but giving the local area more responsibility for the actual distribution of those resources in meeting the priorities of the consumer, the ensuing partnership in decision making can improve the perceived responsiveness of the service.

2.7 Conflict between central control and local autonomy

Diversity in service provision should not be interpreted as total independence of action. Decentralization rightly changes the relationship between front line workers and central management, but in order for diversity to benefit the organization as a whole it needs to be managed. This requires that local managers have sufficient resources and authority to maintain services; that they deliver these within the agreed policy framework of the council; and that communication networks are effective within the organizational structure. The degree of local autonomy for neighbourhood managers should be explicit and not the result of physical isolation, inadequate management or poor communication.

It is argued in the private sector, and increasingly in the public sector as well, that investing local managers with responsibility for their own defined area produces a more satisfied, motivated and therefore efficient worker. But this is not an automatic response to decentralization. Responsibility without authority leads only to frustration in staff and cynicism in consumers.

The conflicts between central and local structures are mirrored by relationships on an intra-departmental level, especially where decentralization has been predominantly single service, housing-led. Becoming more involved with tenants and understanding their problems encourages a different perspective of service delivery. Tenants do not compartmentalize issues according to the niceties of local authority organization. When local housing offices open they are the 'face of the council' and the focus for all problems whether directly housing related or not. Tenants evaluate services on an holistic basis —

litter, poor playground maintenance, or pot holes in the roads all contribute to the quality of life — yet the local housing manager rarely has responsibility for all these issues.

Where the housing department is localized but other complimentary services remain centrally focused, consumers and workers alike can be frustrated by lack of co-ordination and communication. Decentralization has illustrated the problems of limited organizational change of one part without equivalent change in related areas. The case studies illustrated incidences of front line workers developing their own informal networks with workers in other departments at the local level (as a response to this difficulty). Decentralization can be a vehicle for more flexible responsive services but these may develop despite the reorganized structure, rather than as part of the formally revised and agreed procedures.

2.8 Conflict between the established workforce and newly appointed staff

An emphasis on relationships, personal skills and motivation — the human relations aspects of organizational well-being — should be prominent in any balanced analysis. Many proposals to decentralize include an objective to improve the quality and skills of housing staff. To achieve this requires a delicate balance between the utilization of existing staff and the introduction of new talent filling gaps in expertise. However, the value of existing staff resources should not be underestimated. The case studies illustrated how, with support, encouragement and training, many existing staff, currently under-utilized in traditional departments, have often surprised themselves at their ability to take on new tasks and responsibilities.

Despite this there is invariably a need to recruit new staff to meet particular skill shortages or expand the establishment. The influx of newly appointed, often younger, staff to an established workforce of often older workers can produce conflicts and raise issues of the relative importance attached to experience versus qualifications. The values of tradition may conflict with those of professionalism.

These issues are particularly apparent where the middle management level is strengthened with decentralization. We have found the level of area or neighbourhood manager to be crucial to the effectiveness of the local housing service. It is the position with which consumers most readily identify and the person who sets the tone, quality and standard for the service in the locality. This level of management is often new or expanded as a result of decentralization and therefore often one to which new staff are recruited. This provides the opportunity for conflict between new and old which, if unresolved, will obstruct the effective implementation of new systems and working practices.

2.9 Conflict between cultures

This chapter has been concerned, so far, primarily with structural change to organizations, that is changing the framework within which people work and services are provided. But it has been implied that decentralization is about more than this. It has an underlying philosophy concerned with a perception of service delivery that relies on partnership and responsiveness and not uniformity and paternalism. These concepts may be adopted to varying extents throughout the organization. Differences are usually most apparent between the centre and the periphery. In relatively autonomous local offices, often physically isolated from the centre, staff have more opportunity for contact with tenants and become knowledgeable about the area. It is our experience that such staff, often chosen for their commitment to the principles of decentralization, assimilate more readily the culture of decentralization. Faced with the daily reality of tenants' lives, front-line staff adopt a more consumer-led approach to service delivery. At the centre, however, the structural changes brought about by decentralization may not be so apparent. There may be little overt change in their working environment. This disparity in perception of the service can lead to conflict between the neighbourhood and the centre, often exacerbated by lack of communication between the two. Accusations that 'headquarters don't understand the situation we are in — they are out of touch', 'neighbourhood staff just do their own thing, or they bend the rules' are common in some decentralized departments.

Such conflicting views illustrate the need to involve the whole organization when managing radical change. It should be recognized that the centre will also have a new role and new relationships to front-line workers. Training and staff development must take account of changing working environments for all staff within the organization. Decentralization should not simply be concerned with opening additional local offices and dispersing some staff. For effective change all aspects of the organization must be involved — structural and cultural changes must be given equal priority.

> No structure, however well related to the diversity of the environment, will work effectively without a culture appropriate to the structure and people appropriate to the culture, and links between the cultures.
>
> (Handy, 1985)

2.10 The importance of organizational culture

The culture of an organization arises from its values, norms and beliefs. Without change in these, the potential conflicts discussed above are likely to arise as different sections of the organization relate to different cultures. The resolution of many of the problems illustrated by decentralization lies in the extent to which successful cultural change is achieved. The research indicates that structural changes have been more successful than cultural changes, but influences from the private sector have encouraged many authorities to reconsider their priorities.

Decentralized housing organizations can only achieve many of their objectives if they are allowed to become more 'customer driven'. This entails identifying what the customer wants and needs in terms of service delivery, and from that knowledge devising an organizational structure that will enable that form of provision. This has been termed the 'Customer Care' approach to service delivery and owes much to the trends in the private sector promoted by the management 'guru' Tom Peters (Peters and Waterman, 1982). The approach concerns the primacy of the relationship between the consumer and the service at the actual point of delivery. At its simplest, this 'Marks and Spencer approach' involves respecting and valuing staff so that they in turn will be motivated to provide a good service to the customer.

In the private sector such trends in management techniques are generated by market pressures, the profit motive and the need to expand markets. The public sector has traditionally had no such pressure and has been less concerned with the need to maintain market shares. However, in recent years the direction of government housing policy, and public policy in general, has been toward introducing elements of market economics and competition. Through 'Tenants' Choice', encouraging higher rents and compulsory competitive tendering, it is the intention that the pressures which encourage development and change in the private sector will also be felt by the public sector. However, critics of government policy argue that often the public are being given only the illusion of choice, through a dogmatic commitment to market principles in a situation of social polarization and reducing investment.

In such an environment, the philosophy of Customer Care is attractive to many public authorities because it focuses on the consumer and front-line staff and therefore accords well with the culture of decentralization. It is also a management rather than a political force for change, which mirrors the direction of many current decentralization initiatives. Finally, 'Customer care' develops consumerist, individual aspects of service development and delivery, complementing the focus for decentralization which has progressively moved away from the 'collectivist' approach favoured in the early 1980s.

Conclusions

The national provision and management of public-rented housing involves organizations that take a variety of structural forms. Despite the fact that all are performing basically similar functions, there is no one, universally applicable model. The evolution of each organization has been influenced by its specific geographical, social and political environment.

Bureaucratic models have tended to exert greatest influence on local authority housing organizations due to the specific purposes of public-rented housing provision. However, in recent years many councils have begun to reassess their internal structures and their methods of service delivery, partly in response to criticisms of their failings as efficient managers of housing. Many of the criticisms levelled at large housing authorities can be interpreted as criticisms of bureaucratic organization. Responding to such criticisms presents dilemmas for public authorities which seek to retain a rational and impartial method of resource distribution while developing more responsive and personal services.

The principles of decentralization have been widely adopted, but they appear to have been moulded to meet pragmatic, managerial priorities. The adoption of decentralized structures and working practices has had a significant impact but it cannot, and has not, resolved all the problems currently facing local councils. Concentration on structural reorganization alone is not sufficient, 'structural allocation in itself solves few problems, the sinews, nerves, muscles must change with the skeleton' (Handy, 1985). This wider change is more difficult, as it requires an understanding of the stresses imposed by large scale change and a commitment to promote a new organizational culture. This is rarely apparent in practice.

Recently, attempts to extend private market principles to public sector housing have continued to encourage decentralization and given greater priority to the complementary development of a customer-care approach to service delivery.

In conclusion, we would argue that while the influence of decentralization on housing services during the 1980s was considerable, there is now a need to consolidate and extend such trends. It is now the responsibility of councils to consider in what ways their organizations can be improved further in order to maintain services of a quality and quantity expected by their customers. This is no easy task as resources decline and demands increase.

3

Equal opportunities in housing

3.1 Introduction

Equal opportunities considerations are a central aspect of good practice in housing, yet they are rarely given the importance they deserve. Too many housing authorities and associations have realized only in the last few years that they ought to 'do something' about equal opportunities, and have proceeded to adopt an equal opportunities statement and perhaps a tenancy condition prohibiting racial harassment, and have then sat back in the belief that they have a satisfactory policy.

Equal opportunities policies should be targeted at any group that may experience prejudice, disadvantage or discrimination in obtaining housing. This applies to the suitability of the housing they obtain, in their opportunities for peaceful enjoyment of their homes or in gaining employment in housing work. The groups discussed in this chapter include: black and minority ethnic groups*, women, gay men†, and lesbians and disabled people§. They are referred to collectively as target groups.

---

* In most of this chapter the term 'black' is used to refer to all ethnic minority groups who experience discrimination in housing due to their ethnic origins, whatever these origins may be. This usage is current at the time of writing although some people of Asian origin feel that it marginalizes their identity campared with those of Afro-Caribbean origin. It also leaves other groups such as Chinese, Vietnamese, Filipinos and Cypriots in an ambiguous position. Housing organizations are advised to consult the communities they serve on which usage they prefer.

† The term 'gay' is the term preferred by the group to which it refers. Those who complain about the changed meaning of the word lack credibility: they never

This chapter looks first at issues of service delivery to minority ethnic groups, including issues of ethnic monitoring; racial harassment and housing design. It then examines issues of service delivery in relation to women and other target groups. Finally, the issue of equal opportunities in employment is discussed. Inevitably some aspects of the topic will not be fully covered: for a more detailed guide see Dutta and Taylor, 1989.

3.2 Legal position

The position regarding equal treatment of ethnic minorities is set out in the Race Relations Act 1976; for women the relevant Acts are the Sex Discrimination Act 1975 and the Employment Protection Act 1975. There is no law requiring equal treatment, by employers or providers of services, of gay men and lesbians. The notorious Clause 28 of the Local Government Act 1988 prohibits the 'promotion' of homosexuality by local authorities, but should not prevent housing organizations from ensuring that homosexual men and women have equal rights in employment and as users of the housing service.

Employment of disabled people is still governed by the widely criticized Disabled Persons (Employment) Act 1944. This requires employers to ensure that at least three percent of the workforce should be disabled people. Almost no local authorities achieve this requirement: there is a clause that allows them to apply for exemption but this is a disgraceful situation. There is no law requiring equality or preferential treatment in meeting the housing needs of disabled people by housing authorities, although their general duty to meet housing needs may be deemed to include this. The right to adaptations to a dwelling is discussed later.

The Race Relations Act and the Sex Discrimination Act are similar in their intent and effect. They cover employment and the provision of services. Discrimination on grounds of race, sex or marital status is generally illegal, whether direct or indirect (section 3.3 gives definitions). 'Race' is defined to include colour, nationality, ethnic or national origins. Victimization, for example of witnesses, is also illegal. The Race Relations Act also places a duty on local authorities to promote good community relations.

Complaints are made to the Commission for Racial Equality (CRE) or Equal

---

complained so vociferously about the change in meaning of words used with offensive intent such as 'queer'.

§ The British Council of Organizations of Disabled People has adopted the term 'disabled people' in preference to the widely-used 'people with disabilities'. The latter term is seen as focusing on those concerned as having the problem, whereas the problem arises from the way the non-disabled world is arranged so as to exclude them, and from the way others react to physical differences.

Opportunities Commission (EOC) (there is discussion about combining these two bodies). After a thorough investigation the Commission may issue a non-discrimination notice, award compensation and/or recommend action to repair the damage: for example, to offer rehousing or to promote the aggrieved party. A Commission may also initiate an investigation of an organization where it believes discrimination is occurring.

An employer is responsible in law for the actions of an employee and it is no defence that the employer was unaware that discrimination was taking place. The employer has a duty to take steps to ensure that employees do not discriminate: this might include having an equal opportunities policy and procedures backed up with a training programme, clear instructions to staff and a disciplinary procedure for cases where discrimination occurs.

There are a few exceptions to the rules as outlined: employing someone of a particular race or sex may be a genuine occupational requirement, for example, where personal care or language skills are a part of the job, for charities there are also exceptions allowed in service delivery which are particularly relevant to Housing Associations aiming to help particular groups such as homeless Asian women or elderly Turkish Cypriot men (NFHA, 1982), but further advice should be sought to avoid discriminating illegally.

Positive discrimination is illegal: this means giving preference to a member of a group normally subject to less favourable treatment. Positive action is legal: this refers to exceptional measures taken to counteract the effects of past discrimination in order to enable members of target groups to compete more effectively. For example, special training may be provided where a group is underrepresented or absent in the type of work being trained for. This may include promotion opportunities. At the point of selection, however, all candidates must compete on their merits. A later section of this chapter shows how this may be interpreted to place a positive value on the experiences that target groups may bring.

3.3 Definitions

Discrimination may be intentional, but many individuals and organizations behave in ways that result in unequal treatment in spite of intentions or policies for equal treatment. This occurs particularly through stereotyping and institutional discrimination, and to clarify the process it is necessary to define some terms.

Discrimination

Discrimination literally means the perception of differences, but in the equal opportunities context it means worse treatment for a particular group defined by a characteristic such as race, sex or disability. Discrimination may be direct, for example a landlord refusing to let a room to a black tenant, or a housing officer deciding not to register an application from someone in an institution because they do not think the applicant is capable of living independently.

Even if there is no direct discrimination, there may be indirect discrimination if a condition is set that is easier or harder for one group to comply with than another. For example, if an organization said that junior managers must be between 26 and 35 on appointment this would indirectly discriminate against women as a group, in that at these ages they are more likely than men to be out of the labour market in order to care for children.

Racism

This is a belief in the superiority of one race or an assumption that one ethnic group (usually whites) should serve as the norm for other groups. Racism may apply to an attitude or to behaviour. There is some controversy over whether training can, or should, change racist attitudes. Some people believe that attitudes are an individual's business and are not a problem unless linked with racist behaviour; others think that antiracist behaviour is not likely to be sustained in the absence of antiracist attitudes.

Sexism

This is a belief in innately different capacities in men and women as groups, leading to assumptions about appropriate behaviour in the two groups. It generally includes a belief in male superiority. Heterosexism is the assumption that this is the only normal form of sexual behaviour, and the privileging of household forms based on heterosexual relationships. It may be an unconscious bias, a failure to notice that other forms of relationship exist.

There is also institutional racism, sexism and heterosexism. This refers to a situation where an institution is organized around the (usually tacit) assumption that the typical worker or client is white and/or male and/or heterosexual. The formal and informal rules of the organization serve to benefit this group more than others, even though individual workers may not intend to discriminate. For example, rules for rehousing may prioritize married couples with children and relegate other applicants to poorer quality property, or the recruitment process may emphasize achievement in examinations rather than testing for the actual skills needed in the job. We need an '-ism' for the similar set of assumptions that fails to allow for disabled people.

Prejudice

This literally means pre-judgment. In other words, the prejudiced person has a bias against a particular group that is based on a stereotype about that group rather than an evaluation of individual group members. Psychologists believe that contact between groups will reduce prejudice, provided the conditions are such that participants have equal status, if they are cooperating in pursuit of common goals and if there is institutional support for equal treatment (Allport, 1954).

Stereotyping

This is the attribution of particular qualities, behaviours or preferences to a person or group on the basis of a characteristic such as race or sex. For example, a housing worker may assume that an Asian applicant will wish to live near others with the same ethnic origin without asking what he/she really wants. Disability is stereotyped as equating with wheelchair use. Single mothers are assumed not to want to bother with a garden. Indirect and institutional discrimination can often be the result of stereotyping, without conscious intention to treat a group less favourably, or awareness that this is happening. This does not make such treatment any less illegal or offensive to those affected.

Interactions between factors

Some people have more than one of the attributes that are liable to give rise to disadvantage. For example, black women suffer from double discrimination, so too does a disabled gay man. Yet the interaction between different factors is not simply a case of adding them together. Although, for example, women are disadvantaged in most cultures, the disadvantage follows different patterns in different cultures. Racism is gendered; in other words, expectations about women of Caribbean background are different from those about men, and these differences are themselves different from male/female differences in, say, Muslim cultures. Social class and occupation are further mediating factors.

3.3.1 General points

Equal opportunities is an issue arousing strong emotions. This is because equality of treatment is seen as threatening by those who have obtained or hope to obtain positions on the basis of privilege, whilst members of target groups experience discrimination as calling into question their whole social worth. Given that bad practice on equal opportunities is widespread there is a need to move ahead quickly. But it is equally important to be calm and clear about objectives and to consult and inform. New policies and practices must be explained clearly to staff and tenants with the aim of achieving a positive attitude towards the goal of equal treatment.

In the past a double confusion has arisen on the sources of inequality. First, many people who accept that direct discrimination is wrong fail to recognize stereotyping as racist, sexist or in any way discriminatory. An officer who uses his/her judgement about an applicants best interests may see this as proper professional behaviour, not as discrimination. Second, the effect of decisions based on stereotyping or on notions of 'good management practice' in giving rise to bias has been underestimated in comparison with direct discrimination. Thus staff have been angered by accusations of racism without being given an understanding that their own well-intentioned behaviour may constitute indirect discrimination and have an unequal outcome. In particular, the wish to relet voids quickly, and the assumption that certain types of tenant give rise to management problems, are likely to be discriminatory in their effects.

There is controversy on the value of antiracist training in this situation. Such training may serve to reinforce unproductive feelings of guilt. Descriptions of lifestyles and countries of origin of minority groups may merely reinforce stereotypes. Staff may feel defensive and hence resentful and unreceptive, particularly if attendance is compulsory.

The answer is to improve the training, not to eliminate it. In particular there should be careful explanation, using examples, research evidence and skills training, of the problem of stereotyping. It should also be made clear that whatever the personal opinions of staff, their behaviour in the organization must be non-discriminatory and that behaviour to the contrary constitutes misconduct. If there is an issue of possible dismissal, this must be subject to proper procedures and rules of evidence as with any other dismissal for misconduct: this should be explained.

The organization too should be clear on its own stance. It should not allow collective anxiety and guilt at past inequalities to tempt acceptance of unreasonable demands. It is right to regard equality as non-negotiable and to state this for example to groups with fundamentalist beliefs on the inferior status of women. Equal job opportunities does not mean compromises on professional standards, but the organization may need to adapt if its ethos and the demands on job holders are geared to the expectations of white able bodied males.

3.4 The evidence of discrimination

There is considerable evidence of discrimination in housing services against black people but little about other ethnic minorities. There are a few studies on women and some comment, but scant research evidence on the treatment of disabled people and of gay men and lesbians. On equal opportunities in housing employment there is little evidence on the position of any groups apart from women, (on which see Brion and Davies 1984; NFHA, 1984; GLC, 1986; Levison and Atkins, 1987), although it is clear from impression and anecdote that other target groups are far from equally treated. Due to the paucity of material only studies of racial discrimination will be discussed here.

3.4.1 Discrimination on racial grounds

There is ample evidence that ethnic minorities are disadvantaged in all housing tenures (Brown, 1984; DoE 1979). In owner occupied housing they are much more likely than whites to occupy housing in disrepair or lacking amenities, or to be overcrowded. Discrimination by private landlords is well known to occur although it is (usually) illegal. It might be assumed that in the public sector, at least in those authorities professing a commitment to equal opportunities, the situation would be better. In fact, no housing authority that has come under investigation has been found not to be discriminating (CRE, 1984, 1989; Flett, 1981; Henderson and Karn, 1987; Phillips, 1986; Simpson, 1981; Skellington, 1981).

The report of the Cullingworth Committee (Ministry of Housing 1969) on rehousing policies devoted a chapter to a thorough discussion on 'Housing Coloured People'. The report pointed out that although local authorities without exception claimed to operate in a 'colour-blind' manner, several factors meant that ethnic minorities were failing to benefit from council housing. They advocated keeping ethnic records to ensure that treatment is indeed equal and that needs are being met. The Association of Metropolitan Authorities (AMA 1985) 16 years later recommended that local authorities now implement Cullingworth's advice: a sign of the extraordinary lack of priority with which most authorities treat equal opportunities issues.

Earlier, a number of studies showed that ethnic minority households were being denied their fair share of council housing (Burney, 1967; Rex and Moore, 1967; Daniel 1968; Smith and Whalley, 1975). Between 1974 and 1982 the proportion of West Indians in council housing had risen from 26% to 44%, and of Asians from 4% to 18% (Brown, 1984). If access to the tenure is improving, albeit into worse quality property than whites, this is not so much due to deliberate changes in policy by local authorities as to changes in government policy towards the public sector. Increasingly, this is seen as a tenure of last resort for those outside the labour market, rather than a good quality provision for a substantial proportion of the population (see Willmott and Murie, 1988). The price of admission has been residualization.

Council housing is allocated by different means from one authority to another, but they all have in common a stock of varying desirability and a diverse group of applicants with different degrees of urgency of housing need, and thus different abilities to wait for the type of property they really want.

Several studies have shown how applicants with greatest need tend to be allocated the worst accommodation (see for example Clapham and Kintrea, 1986). Black households in the private sector tend to be in worse conditions than whites, so their greater need is one reason why they are likely to find themselves in less desirable council properties. However, the studies published in the 1980s cited above have shown that there are differences which cannot be explained in this way: there is very strong evidence of, at best, indirect discrimination and institutional racism.

All this work has shown that black households receive less than their share of good quality property, although the definition of what was less or more desirable varied with the locality. In most areas, older property was seen as inferior to new (and was disproportionately allocated to black households, especially Asians), but in Nottingham, where new property took the form of an unpopular large concrete deck access scheme, it was here that black households tended to be concentrated.

The studies cited were careful in their methodology to exclude causes for different treatment other than discrimination. Part of the difference encountered could in some studies be attributed to factors such as rehousing route (waiting list, transfer, slum clearance, homelessness, rehabilitation of existing dwelling), family size or type, preferences of applicants or availability of stock. In some cases, controlling for these factors revealed that discrimination was *worse* than aggregated figures showed. For example Asian families may have been offered fewer houses than whites but taking their larger average family size into account should have been offered more.

Henderson and Karn's study (1987) was particularly thorough, and disturbing in its findings. The authority studied, Birmingham, operated a points system, but for every type of property black households had more points at the time of rehousing than whites — in other words, their housing need was greater. The research included observation in the housing department, and the authors show that officer discretion may be exercised at many points in the rehousing process, usually (unconsciously) to the detriment of black households. The different ethnic groups did tend to be concentrated in different areas of Birmingham and the pattern of locational choices made by rehousing applicants roughly corresponded to these, but the allocations showed a greater tendency towards concentration than the choices: thus opportunities for dispersal by choice were not being taken.

The CRE study of Hackney resulted in a non-discrimination notice being served. Hackney had been chosen virtually at random and co-operated with the investigation; the CRE believed that the findings could be replicated in any other London borough and probably in any authority where there is an ethnic minority community. Some authorities did review their procedures following the Hackney study, but a survey of 61 authorities by the AMA in 1985 found only a third were keeping ethnic records on applications and fewer than this monitored any other aspect of service delivery. The number where the outcome was reported to committee, or the policy changed as a result of monitoring, was even fewer.

Few Housing Associations can afford to be complacent about their performance in this area, although the NFHA has given an earlier lead than the local authority associations. Their publications (1982, 1983 and 1985), especially the first, offer excellent guidance in this area, with relevance for local authorities as well as the voluntary sector. Niner's study (1985) of Housing Association allocations in the West Midlands is also interesting. All these studies recommend ethnic monitoring and some include guidance on how to carry it out. The CRE's Code of Practice (CRE, 1991) applies to all housing organizations.

3.5 Service delivery: ethnic minorities

3.5.1 Ethnic monitoring

Virtually every report that has considered the issue seriously has stressed the importance of ethnic monitoring. Study after study has shown that the 'colour-blind' approach is ineffective in securing equal treatment. There are several points of 'good practice' in relation to ethnic monitoring.

The ethnic minority communities in the area served must be involved in the recommendation to undertake monitoring and in decisions on how to monitor. Wherever possible the categorizing of an ethnic group should be made by the individual concerned rather than being based on an assessment by a housing officer. Data on ethnic identity of individuals should only be used for the purposes for which it is collected and should never be passed to third parties. This must be made clear at the point of collection.

There is no single 'correct' set of categories: this will depend on the size of the organization, the size and make-up of the local ethnic minority population and their own views on the matter. Any groups whose members feel themselves to be disadvantaged or subject to discrimination should be included as a category, including white minorities such as Irish, Greek or Turkish Cypriot if they are present in significant numbers locally. All these are included in Haringey's ethnic monitoring categories. The NFHA suggests 2% of the population in the area as a suitable threshhold, but organizations should consult as widely as possible, and certainly include any smaller groups that request this.

There are differing views on whether ethnic data should be stored in such a way that they are clear to anyone using the records, or in some coded form that can only be used by those analysing the monitoring. Generally the latter is likely to demotivate staff by making them fearful that they may find themselves criticized for unwitting discrimination. A better approach is to build consensus on equal opportunities goals through training, discussion and a positive lead from managers, then allow staff the information they need to achieve equality objectives.

One of the difficulties encountered in monitoring allocations is how to measure the quality of property offered. Some monitoring schemes have failed due to an over elaborate or contentious system. A possible scheme is given in NFHA (1985) which could be adapted to particular circumstances. It is not to be expected that each ethnic group will be exactly proportionately represented in each category as different groups may place different values on the various attributes of a dwelling.

One possibility is to look at allocation outcomes in relation to choices, but the pattern of choices must also be monitored. If minority households are expressing choices for lower quality property, are these choices being distorted by urgency of need, lack of awareness of alternatives, fear of racial violence in certain areas, or any other factors indicating that the organization should review its policies and practices? Simpson (1981) discusses how different groups have varying scope for choice due in part to such factors, but also because for white households a location near their family and friends and the facilities they value is compatible with good quality property, whereas other ethnic groups may have to choose between family, friends and facilities on the one hand and good quality property on the other.

Ethnic monitoring is not an end in itself. The results must be analysed: if they demonstrate bias the reasons for this must be carefully considered. There may have been direct discrimination by an individual: if so this is clearly a serious matter and the source must be traced. However, bias often arises through factors built into the system (institutional racism) and could thus indicate a need for policy changes. Goodwill towards equal opportunities policies will be lost if staff feel at risk of personal criticism or disciplinary action when it is actually the policies which are at fault.

Evidence of systematic bias should be reported to committee and remedies discussed with community organizations, tenants' organizations and housing staff. It is important in such discussions to make clear what scope for intervention is being offered. The policy goal (equality) is not open to debate, but the means of implementing it is.

Organizations must consider carefully what aspects of service delivery to monitor: too often it is limited to allocations. Other potential areas include:

• requests for assessment for medical priority;
• cases where medical priority is granted;
• waiting list applications;
• transfer applications;
• transfers effected;

- homelessness applications;
- acceptances as homeless;
- outcomes of acceptance, e.g. use of temporary accommodation as opposed to direct rehousing or remaining in existing situation;
- requests for 'special case' consideration or Councillor cases;
- proportion of the above that are successful;
- repair requests;
- speed and standard of completion of repairs;
- improvement grant applications;
- improvement grants given;
- housing benefit claims.

Although this may seem a long list, all the items mentioned can be sources of unequal treatment between groups and it is the duty of housing organizations to treat all sections of the community equally.

Particular care is needed in introducing monitoring of benefit claims due to the false but common portrayal by the press of black claimants as being prone to make fraudulent claims. In fact it is more likely that black people are under-claiming through lack of information about entitlement. Monitoring might be accompanied by a take-up campaign with information available in minority languages* and it is important that housing officers fully understand the benefit regulations: for example, some people are only admitted to the UK on condition that they do not have recourse to public funds.

There is insufficient experience on how to avoid or remedy bias in most of the areas listed above, since so few of them are monitored by any housing organization at present that practice guidelines have not yet developed. Once monitoring has demonstrated the existence of a problem, solutions are likely to emerge through discussions with the ethnic groups affected, tenants and staff.

On allocations there is considerable research evidence which shows that the following factors tend to result in unequal treatment:

- a residence qualification (that is, a certain period of residence required prior to registration or to rehousing);
- rules disadvantageous to single men;
- rules requiring children to reside with the applicant in order to qualify for family accommodation;
- worse treatment for cohabitees than for married couples;
- worse treatment of single parents than two-parent families;
- preference to sons and daughters of existing tenants;

---

* It is important that translations of documents should be available but their value should not be overestimated: many people who cannot read English are illiterate in their mother tongue. Other alternatives such as audio tapes might be considered.

- rules prohibiting two households from being rehoused together even if this is their preference;
- a shortage of larger properties;
- one-offer-only policy for homeless households;
- restrictions on eligibility for transfers, or poor information on how to transfer, or excessive weight given to medical needs;
- excessive officer discretion;
- excessive scope for Councillors or committee members to give priority to exceptional cases outside the normal rules.

3.5.2 Harassment

Racial harassment must be broadly defined: it may include graffiti, violence or intimidation, verbal abuse, damage to property, noise, arson, false accusations to third parties, intimidation by dogs or other animals, depositing offensive substances and so on. It differs from most neighbour disputes, which usually involve anti-social behaviour carried out with indifference as to who suffers or is sometimes directed at a particular neighbour as a vendetta. Harassment is usually unprovoked or is totally disproportionate to any initiating act.

Unfortunately there is no specific law against racial harassment. Some housing organizations have written a clause prohibiting harassment into their tenancy conditions, and 'conduct which is a nuisance or annoyance to neighbours' is a statutory ground for possession. In practice it is easier to use this ground in possession proceedings than any clause on harassment, since the latter will require that the landlord demonstrates that the perpetrator had racism as a motive.

Before any action can be taken on harassment the housing organization must create the climate of opinion where victims of harassment will come forward to report incidents, knowing both that the incident will be investigated properly and that they will be supported and protected if necessary. The victim should have the right to see a housing officer of the same race if they wish. The housing officer seeing them should have an awareness of support groups available and should ask the victim if he/she wishes to be put in touch with them.

The aim of policy should be to stop the perpetrators from continuing their harassment and to ensure that all types of household can safely occupy any part of the stock. Eviction of perpetrators is not a goal in itself but may be a policy of last resort in order to allow peaceful occupation by the household that has been victimized and to make it clear to perpetrators and to the ethnic minority community that the organization is determined to put a stop to harassment. No action should be taken that is contrary to the wishes of the victim, for example involving police or going to court to seek possession.

The housing service or community workers should work with tenants' groups, to ensure that they do not condone harassment or discrimination and to also involve them in action against perpetrators (for example, as witnesses). Climate of opinion may be as effective a deterrent as the threat of legal action.

Sometimes the victims will wish to move for their own safety, although sometimes only temporary accommodation is needed. The victim's need to move must be accepted even though it may appear a victory to the perpetrators. If the vacated property is later offered to another household at risk of harassment, they should be told why it became vacant and be given the chance to refuse the offer without prejudicing any future offers. If the victim wishes to remain in the property there are various measures that can be taken to protect them, such as security locks, fireproof letterboxes and alarm systems.

There is an excellent guide to legal action on racial harassment (Forbes, 1988) which deals with the subject in far more detail than is possible here. It would also help anyone dealing with harassment on grounds other than race; no housing office should be without it.

3.5.3 Design, newbuild, rehabilitation

It is impossible to achieve racial equality in service delivery if the quantity and quality of the stock do not allow it. Property designed with the indigenous population in mind will not necessarily be suitable for other lifestyles, and the pattern of household sizes may be different. Consultation with users is vital, as lifestyles are changing for all groups and it is easy for designers to operate with a set of stereotyped images that are inappropriate to the actual clients concerned.

At present the average household size for some Asian groups is higher than for whites, in part because a high proportion are at the stage in the life cycle where children are at home, but also because average numbers of children are higher (Brown, 1984). This may be a temporary pattern but some other ethnic groups, for example orthodox Jews, have chosen to maintain their tradition for large families over several generations. Another family pattern common in Asian households is the extended family living under one roof (Brown, 1984). This is partly through choice and partly constraint; again it may, or may not, change over time.

Many writers on ethnic groups have commented on the greater acceptability of single parenthood among people of Caribbean origin. Although there are many black single parent families, attitudes to single parenthood are changing very rapidly among white groups, and within both groups there is a wide spread of attitudes ranging from strictness to permissiveness. Single parenthood is taboo for most Asian families and this may suggest a greater need for accommodation for single Asian women who do break these norms.

Any statistical differences between groups such as those outlined above may or may not apply in particular cases. Housing staff must be aware of cultural patterns but must be careful not to make stereotyped assumptions based on the client's skin colour.

There is a need for more information on the design needs of different groups but a few pointers can be given. In some cultures men and women will socialize separately, so two living spaces of reasonable size are required (one might be a large kitchen). It may be a religious requirement to wash under running water, so showers and mixer taps will be needed. During Ramadan, food may be prepared very late at night or early in the morning: if Muslim families have to be given temporary accommodation in hotels or bed and breakfast, there must be appropriate facilities to allow observance of religious or dietary rules. Some groups, for example orthodox Jews, may have particular requirements on arrangements for food preparation.

In any consultation with user groups on design it must be made clear how much scope for choice there is, and what are the constraints of cost, time and procedures. If people are unaccustomed to have their views sought, the hardest task may be to get them first to conceptualize and then articulate their real preferences. If consultation can be undertaken by a member of staff who shares the ethnic origin of the consultees this may facilitate the process.

Many of the recommendations made in a later section relating to design and safety for women will also help people from ethnic minority groups who are at risk of racially-motivated attack.

3.6 Service delivery: women

Compared with the evidence on racial discrimination, there is almost no material on sex discrimination in service delivery. Households headed by women are disproportionately represented in the public sector, but unlike the CRE, the EOC has shown no interest in whether discrimination is occurring. (This is changing: the EOC and Shelter have recently funded a research project on women's housing experiences. Research is also in progress at the Women's Design Service on the housing needs of older women.)

As we have seen, the practice of ethnic monitoring is extremely patchy and partial, but gender monitoring is virtually unheard of. In the absence of evidence it is safe to assume that gender-blind policies are no more successful in creating equality of treatment than colour-blind policies.

Women are not a minority but the majority of the population. Their needs are not all alike: women may want housing with or without partners, they may be lesbian or heterosexual, with children or childfree, elderly or not, with disabilities or not, black or white. This section will try to pinpoint some of the circumstances in women's lives where they may have particular needs and to highlight some design issues important to all women.

For most young single women living with their parent(s) or in someone else's household it is extremely difficult to acquire a home of their own. They are very unlikely to have sufficient income to buy and are seen as having low priority by most local authorities and housing associations. Re-housing may be needed at short notice as a result of a crisis: for example sexual abuse or being asked to leave after becoming pregnant or 'coming out' as a lesbian.

A confirmed pregnancy should mean that the local authority accepts repsonsibility for rehousing, but only a few authorities regard lesbians as 'vulnerable' and offer rehousing on these grounds. A woman who has been sexually abused may be hesitant at explaining the reason for her housing need. It is important that all women clients have the opportunity to see a women member of staff if they wish, and that staff are trained in how to assess sensitive situations. Staff are there to address the housing need rather than deal with personal problems, but they must have an awareness of the way these factors interact and must know how to refer clients to support groups or professional help if necessary.

There are strong arguments for regarding any single homeless woman as vulnerable and offering rehousing. Some young women may need housing because they have come from local authority care rather than a parental home. Any young person in their first independent home may require support and advice, especially if they have had less opportunity to learn how to run a home because of being in care. Tenancy support workers can provide help, and policies should not debar a person from future rehousing if a tenancy has failed, leaving arrears outstanding.

Local authorities may often offer single pregnant women and single mothers flats rather than houses; in part because this may be the most readily available accommodation where needs are urgent, but there may also be stereotyping or punitive attitudes. It may be that the applicant prefers re-housing in a flat to temporary bed and breakfast accommodation. The best practice is to explain options clearly, avoid stereotyping, listen to the wishes of the applicant, and to aim for equal treatment regardless of marital status.

3.6.1 Sole or joint tenant

Where a woman is rehoused with a partner, the current conventional wisdom is that they should be joint tenants. This is usually prefereable to the old fashioned practice where the tenancy was held in the husband's name, but there are certain disadvantages.

First, joint tenants are each potentially responsible for the total sum of any arrears. This may mean that a woman whose partner has left and who had no means of paying while he was resident or until the tenancy is put into her sole name, is nonetheless required to pay off the debt incurred by the partner. The landlord should use discretion to write off any arrears that cannot be recovered from the former partner in such circumstances. Second, it may be easier for the woman to get a partner to leave if necessary, for example if he is violent, if she is sole tenant. Thus if a household includes children who are dependents of the woman but not her partner, she might be advised to have the tenancy in her sole name. She may of course still choose a joint tenancy.

Same-sex partners should always be joint tenants unless there are exceptional circumstances, as only this can ensure that a surviving partner can succeed to the tenancy in the same way as a surviving spouse. A heterosexual cohabitee is normally regarded as a member of the late tenant's family for succession purposes.

3.6.2 Relationship breakdown

Housing organizations should not see it as part of their role to keep couples together where one partner wishes to leave, for example by insisting on a certain period of separation before rehousing can be considered. Procedures in the event of relationship breakdown will differ according to:

• whether or not there has been violence;
• whether the parties are joint tenants, and if not, which party holds the tenancy;
• whether or not there are dependent children.

In cases of violence, the first priority must be the safety of the victim. She may need temporary accommodation or immediate rehousing away from the violent partner. A woman in fear of violence should be accepted as genuinely homeless and not required to seek an injunction before her case is dealt with. If it is necessary to obtain supporting evidence this can be done once she has moved. Neighbours, or the allegedly violent partner, should never be asked to corroborate the woman's account (Welsh Women's Aid, 1986).

Refuges run by groups affiliated to the Women's Aid Federation provide valuable support to women escaping from violence, and may be more acceptable to users than a facility run by the local authority. However, there must be good liaison on policies for rehousing to ensure that places in the refuge are not blocked by women being forced to stay there for months on end (Women's Aid Federation, 1981). Some ethnic minority women are reluctant to use mixed race refuges due to fears or reports of racism. Obviously refuges should try to make women of all races feel welcome and secure, but it may also be worth considering funding specialized provision where, say, Asian women can receive support from women of a similar cultural background.

A woman who is a joint tenant may terminate the tenancy on guarantee of rehousing, and the violent partner can then be evicted. However, it is possible that the evicted tenant would then be able to sue the joint tenant for breach of trust. The woman should be offered the choice between returning to the previous home or the offer of another property of similar quality. Some housing authorities will not rehouse the partner where there is proof of violence such as an injunction or conviction for assault. If the partner is sole tenant a battered woman may still have rights to the home, and to an injunction excluding the partner. If she is sole tenant she should get legal advice on how to remove the unwanted partner. Violence from outside the home is discussed in the section on harassment.

In non-violent cases of relationship breakdown of joint tenants, the parties may be able to agree on who should keep the tenancy. If there are children the party who has care of them will usually stay in the existing home, and the other party is entitled to rehousing. However, this should not be a rigid rule: a woman who wishes to leave a relationship may not wish to compound the partner's problems by making him leave the home. In such cases it is wrong to regard the woman as 'not genuinely homeless' on the grounds that he is willing for her to return (Brailey, 1986).

If the woman is sole tenant she is entitled to require a cohabitee to leave but should seek legal advice on how to do this. If she is asked to leave by a partner who is sole tenant she is threatened with homelessness. If the couple are married she has rights in the home and should seek legal advice. Otherwise rehousing should be automatic if there are dependent children. Even without children there may be vulnerability factors which would lead the local authority to offer rehousing.

3.6.3 Succession of carers

A spouse takes precedence in succeeding to a tenancy on the death of a tenant, and then a member of the tenant's family resident for at least the year before the death. This may disqualify succession by someone (usually a woman) who has recently moved in (or back) to care for the tenant, possibly giving up her own home to do so. Under the 1988 Housing Act there is a two-year qualifying period of residence for a relative other than a spouse to succeed to a statutory tenancy (that is, tenancies in privately rented or Housing Association accommodation which were protected tenancies prior to the 1988 Housing Act). Even then the successor becomes an assured tenant, with higher rent and reduced security. Non-relatives have no succession rights at all. Housing Associations' and local authorities' policies must recognize the needs of carers; they should consider making a grant of tenancy on terms of parity with secure tenants, where the carer is not entitled to succeed to the tenancy.

3.6.4 Design

Architects tend to operate with an image of the 'typical' family: in fact a television advert stereotype hardly found in real life. It would be better to concentrate on the need for a building to offer a framework for many different lifestyles. A family size house may be occupied by a two parent or one parent family or by adult sharers; children of the tenant may be babies, teenagers or well into middle age, living with elderly parents. Household members may choose to spend most of their spare time together or may each follow individual activities in different rooms — but many homes are planned around an assumed collective 'family life' and fail to provide for individual privacy. Even smaller dwellings must accommodate a variety of lifestyles. A couple of whatever age may not wish to spend every minute together and may each want a room of their own.

Despite changes in gender roles, women still do by far the major part of the housework, childcare and cooking in most homes. Now that most women also have paid jobs it is particularly important that the home is designed to facilitate these tasks. In the words of the Parker Morris report, the home 'must be something of which (people) can be proud, and in which they must be able to express the fullness of their lives ... stress will be laid upon quality rather than mere adequacy' (Ministry of Housing and Local Government, 1961). Maintaining a home may be experienced as burdensome but it may also be a valued means of self-expression, a source of positive feelings about (literally) one's place in the world.

The neighbourhood must be designed with women's safety in mind. This will include good lighting, routes from the public street or bus stop to the front door that can be surveyed before use, secure doors and windows, layouts that deter non-residents from loitering. Various recent studies give further advice, some including examples of good and bad practice (Boys, 1984; Southwark, 1984; Ware, 1988.) Any programme of estate improvements should involve consultation with residents, and some women-only meetings should be held to discuss the issues that concern them times convenient to them. Since black people are also at risk of attack, they too may be able to state their needs more freely in separate meetings.

Most elderly people and disabled people are women. The needs of elderly people are not discussed here as a number of specialized guides are available; the needs of disabled people are discussed below.

3.6.5 Harassment due to sex, sexuality or disability

A woman living without a male partner is sometimes victimized by neighbours seeing her as 'fair game', and may receive obscene suggestions, nuisance callers, telephone calls or actual or threatened violence. These become more likely if her behaviour does not conform to what her neighbours think is proper, for example if she has a woman partner, a black partner or several men friends. Women are also at risk of violence from ex-partners no longer living with them, or associates or relatives of ex-partners. Gay men are often harassed due to prejudice or fear of AIDS (which is simply a cover for prejudice, as there is no real risk to a neighbour of an AIDS sufferer). Disabled people may be harassed merely because they are different and are not usually able to defend themselves. Far fewer housing organizations have procedures for dealing with these types of harassment than for racial harassment. In the absence of a body of opinion on 'good practice' many of the guidelines given earlier on racial harassment may be used. For example, there should be a victim-centred approach; the safety of the victim must be the first concern; action should not go beyond what the victim wishes; the desire for rehousing should be accepted; referral to a support group should be offered; any chance of making it clear to perpetrators that their behaviour is unacceptable should be taken (unless the victim doesn't want this). Again eviction may be considered if warnings have proved ineffective, and attempts should be made to create a climate of opinion where threats, violence and offensive behaviour to others is clearly regarded as wrong.

3.7 Disabled people

Like women and ethnic minorities, disabled people are the subject of stereotypes about the sort of housing they need. There are many different types of disability and design needs are totally different in each case: consider the cases of a partially sighted person, an amputee, someone who has learning difficulties and someone with AIDS. Some of these may live alone, some with family members or with others who may or may not have disabilities themselves. A recent government study showed that as many as one in ten of the population have disabilities, and that two thirds of these are elderly. The vast majority live in private households rather than institutions (OPCS, 1988).

It is often forgotten that disabled people are not all white, or when this is realized the needs of disabled black people are not often properly investigated: it is either assumed that these needs are the same as whites' or that 'their own people' will take care of them. Either of these *may* be true but they must be investigated, not assumed.

There is a useful review of research and information on local authority provision of housing services for disabled people by Keeble (1983). This shows the inadequacy of information on special housing needs in most local authorities. Information quickly becomes out of date due to people newly becoming disabled, moving into or out of institutions, deaths or migration. Two reports by Shelter (1988, 1990) confirm this dismal picture. Keeble advocates a special register: as well as acting as a guide to specialized requirements in newbuild accommodation this would improve reletting of units that fall vacant. GPs, voluntary groups and Social Services departments may be good sources of information on unmet needs. Since disabled people may have more precise requirements than other applicants it is good practice to allow unlimited offers rather than the usual limit on numbers of offers that may be refused.

Local authorities could do very much more to provide tailor-made accommodation, designed with the participation of future tenants. A proportion of any new housing should be purpose-designed for disabled people. It is not sufficient to assume that disability equates with wheelchair or mobility housing. Specialized design guides (Islington Council, 1989; Penton and Barlow, 1980; Thorpe, 1985) must be used so that common faults are avoided.

A high proportion of two and three bedroom units will allow more flexibility in allocations. Underoccupation should be accepted: many disabled people will have carers living with them for some of the time, or will need a live-in carer in future. Too large a proportion of purpose-built accommodation has only one bedroom: in fact the mix of sizes will need to be at least as wide as for other groups. It should not be assumed that non-disabled household members will automatically provide any care that is needed: extra space for a carer may be needed even in larger households.

Many design features aimed to help occupiers with a disability will improve a dwelling's amenity for all users: for example, electric sockets set well above floor level, good illumination, wider doorways and passageways, non-slip flooring, room for manoeuvre in bathrooms and kitchens, accessible meters and stop taps, straight flight stairs. It must also be remembered that able-bodied people may be visited by disabled friends.

Decisions on whether to move into purpose-built accommodation or to remain in the existing home with adaptations or in an institution should always rest with the individual (and others in his/her household if applicable) after discussions of options with occupational therapists (OT), technical and housing officers. It is not the job of a housing officer to make such decisions on behalf of a disabled person. New technologies such as remote control press button alarms can allow people to live independently where this would previously have carried high risks.

Those who need them in whatever tenure have the right to disabled adaptations to their existing home. These should have very high priority in expenditure decisions: if possible there should be no ceiling on spending on an individual property or overall. Unfortunately under the 1989 Local Government and Housing Act disabled facilities grants are subject to a means test. This gives rise to delay and some householders may be deterred from carrying out necessary adaptations. Other common causes of delay are: the shortage of OTs, poor co-ordination between housing and social services departments, delays in drawing up schemes, planning permission, obtaining committee approval, the tender process and unreliability of builders, obtaining consents from private landlords. One department, say housing, should take a lead in suggesting procedures for speeding up all these processes, using delegated authority as much as possible and ensuring that all concerned are committed to making these procedures work.

In order to allow ordinary participation in social life by disabled people, all housing should be designed to accommodate a wide cross-section of the population. The environment should be barrier-free, with sufficient width in doorways, circulation areas and manoeuvering spaces for those with mobility impairments, and meeting the 'visitability' standard of a downstairs WC in every house.

There are other housing management issues related to disability. Harassment sometimes occurs and clear rules and guidelines are needed on dealing with perpetrators. Disabled people who become homeless will usually qualify for rehousing as vulnerable. There should be common objectives and clarity about working together from housing and social services departments and health authorities, particularly where institutions are being closed and their residents rehoused in 'the community'. 'Community Care' will place new duties on housing and social services authorities and a specialized guide should be consulted (for example, Harrison and Means, 1990). Some of these issues are discussed in more detail in Chapters 4 and 5.

3.8 Unacceptable behaviour by housing workers

Employees of an organization may harass or show bias against particular tenants or fellow workers on grounds of race, sex, sexuality or disability. Examples might be:

- a housing officer denied promotion because he/she rejected the sexual approaches of a senior;
- a rehousing officer saying to a lesbian couple 'we couldn't put you on that estate, the neighbours wouldn't tolerate it';
- an employee with noticeable disabilities being denied the chance to do work bringing him into contact with the public because his manager thought people would be upset;
- housing benefit claims from people with Asian surnames being left until last, or more detailed proof of financial circumstances being required than for white claimants;
- a black tenant repeating a repair request being given racist verbal abuse and accused of being over-demanding;
- colleagues of a gay man asking for him to be suspended due to fear of AIDS.

There must be no collusion with such behavior. The accuser (who might be the victim or a colleague who has observed unacceptable behaviour) must be given support and must be confident that the matter will be thoroughly investigated. She/he may need help in presenting a case. The investigation should be carried out by someone in a senior position in another part of the organization (for example, a manager in another area office who does not work closely with either party). This investigation should aim at ascertaining all relevant facts and circumstances; a report should then go to the Director who will make a decision on what action to take.

The trade union has a part to play in ensuring that the investigation is fairly carried out and that any disciplinary action is commensurate with the offence. There is, however, a difference between the proper defence of a member's interests and culpable failure to recognize the seriousness of racism, sexism and other forms of discrimination.

3.8.1 Prejudice or abuse from tenants towards housing workers

Because of the hierarchical structure of housing departments and the institutionalized racism and sexism in society, it will often be women and/or ethnic minority staff who occupy positions where they are in the front line of contact with the public. Such staff must be able to feel confident that the organization will not tolerate prejudiced behaviour from clients. Real examples encountered in housing work include:

- a tenant who has had to wait for a repair or for rehousing alleges that he would have received this service more quickly if he had been black;
- the advice of a woman or ethnic minority housing officer is not believed and the client asks to see someone in authority;
- a tenant mimics the accent or stance of a worker who differs from the norm;
- sexual innuendo towards women staff.

It must be made clear to the client that this type of behaviour is offensive and unjustified. If the client persists the interview should be terminated. It is important that a white/male/heterosexual/able-bodied worker should not let a prejudiced remark pass as this colludes with the client's prejudice. Sometimes the worker who has been given offence can make it clear to the client that his/her behaviour is unacceptable, but at other times he/she will ask the manager to take action, by writing to or interviewing the client.

3.9 Employment issues

Even though this textbook is directed at housing workers in the early stages of their career, guidelines on equal opportunities in recruitment and employment are relevant. A junior member of staff may still be able to make suggestions through his/her manager which will get taken up by those in decision-making positions, or members of staff may get together to press for, say, improved promotion prospects for black staff or better nursery provision. They may be able to use the trade union to push the organization towards a more thorough implementation of equal opportunities in recruitment and employment practice.

Some excellent guides on employment of target groups are available, including Palmer and Poulton's *Sex and Race Discrimination in Employment* (1987), the NFHA's *Race and Housing: Employment and Training Guide* (1989) and Kettle and Massie's *Employer's Guide to Disabilities* (1986). The latter describes how thirty different conditions may affect a person's capacities or needs as a worker as well as giving general guidance on the law, available help and good practice.

The following are points for consideration on good practice in general. Some of them are already standard practice in progressive housing organizations but the author is not aware of any organization where all, or even a significant majority, of the points are practised.

1. Posts should be openly advertised: 'slotting in' or recruitment by word of mouth is incompatible with equal opportunities. It is however acceptable for an organization to offer temporary 'acting rank' promotions to cover absences such as secondments or maternity/paternity leave to members of target groups in order to develop skills and experience.
2. All members of a selection panel should have received training in equal opportunities in recruitment practice.
3. All recruitment and selection panels should be mixed in race and gender. If there are no women or black employees in suitable positions to act as recruiters, or so few that recruitment threatens to take an undue proportion of their time, consider bringing in, for example, existing staff at the same level as the vacancy, councillors or members of a central personnel team, external consultants or members of local organizations such as a Community Relations Council.
4. All members of the recruitment panel should be involved in decisions on the qualities being sought and the selection criteria, the wording of any advertisement, shortlisting, questions to be asked at interview and any other selection procedures. It is tokenism for most of these steps to be carried out by an unrepresentative group which then invites a target group member to join them for the actual interviews.
5. In considering what qualities, experience or qualifications are needed in the job, do not rely on exam qualifications or a conventional career path; define the qualities required in the work and examine whether candidates possess them. For example, many disabled people and black people have

had a poor deal from the education system and may have underachieved at school. If, say, the ability to write clear reports is required, assess this from the application form or set a test rather than requiring a GCSE in English. Similarly, relevant voluntary work, informal advice-giving in the community or direct experience of housing problems may be as valuable as actual housing work. Ensure that the job advert makes it clear that such experience is taken into account.

6. Consider advertising in a range of outlets including the ethnic press, talking newspapers, social centres catering for particular groups and so on. (However, some organizations have found that multiple advertising is not cost effective and may be seen as patronizing: after all most potential candidates in target groups will read the mainstream press for job adverts.)

7. Advertisements should go beyond the now conventional claim that the organization considers all applications equally, to give more detail on why applications from target groups are particularly welcome: for example because they are underrepresented at this level, or to improve services to the whole community.

8. If insufficient numbers from the target groups apply for a job, particularly if any group is underrepresented in that type of post, the job should be readvertised with the wording amended to make it clear why this is being done.

9. There is no firm evidence that members of any target group are more prone than white, able-bodied heterosexual males to take sickleave, arrive late, move jobs or take other action that may be a problem to the employer. There is some evidence that once recruited, disabled employees are likely to give long service (Kettle and Massie, 1986) (point 20 also.).

10. Consider guaranteeing an interview to any disabled applicant unless he or she is obviously unsuitable.

11. It should go without saying that women candidates are never asked questions about their plans to marry or have children or their arrangements for child care. Even if male candidates are asked similar questions, replies from women tend to be invested with different significance.

12. Ask all candidates questions to ascertain their commitment to equal opportunities policies, and to ensure that they are aware of the range of target groups involved.

13. The interviewers should independently assess all candidates according to the criteria agreed at the start, and then confer on their assessments. If two candidates appear equally suitable, consider taking 'positive action' by giving preference to a member of a target group.

14. Selectors should be accountable: unsuccessful candidates should be able to enquire through another channel (such as a personnel officer) why they were not selected. If the panel has kept proper records of their decisions,

for example scoring systems, they can justify their decision without feeling threatened and also offer constructive feedback.

15. Consider liaising with the Disablement Resettlement Officer and Disablement Advisory Service with a view to adapting the job to the skills of the person rather than vice versa. For example, an applicant might be offered a job on a special job description combining those parts of several jobs which his/her abilities allowed.

16. Recognize that enabling a disabled person to do all aspects of a job description as written may involve expense (adapting access to workplaces, modifying internal layouts, employing readers or signers, purchase of special equipment and so on). Equal opportunities policies cannot be implemented at nil cost. Grants are available for the capital cost of adaptations, but only for a named disabled employee rather than for general improvements to accessibility.

17. Provide opportunities for career progression for disabled employees as for other workers. It is invidious to assume that such an employee will be grateful for a job and should not expect a career.

18. Equal opportunities for women cannot be achieved without adequate child care provision and job share opportunities at all levels. Such facilities should be available to employees of both sexes.

19. Black staff should not be ringfenced into posts where there is a community relations component. Ensure that black staff get a range of mainstream experience to prepare them to take up middle or senior management positions.

20. Generalizations about characteristics of a group must not be made on the basis of an individual's performance. For example, if a member of a particular group is a poor manager or has a chip on their shoulder this must not be assumed to be typical of that group.

21. Positive action may be taken in offering training opportunities to members of target groups to help them compete for senior posts if (as is usually the case) they are underrepresented in such posts. For example, they may be given priority for day release to gain qualifications.

22. Someone who is the first (or second or third) of their group in a post may need extra support to be effective. One possibility is to encourage self-development groups, for example for women managers. Black and ethnic minority staff may wish to form a group to discuss issues of common concern. Line managers should allow reasonable time off for such groups to meet and should ensure that support and training needs are being met.

23. Even if recruitment is well-balanced (with new staff at each level roughly in proportion to corresponding groups in the local population) the workforce will not be representative if target group members leave at a greater rate than others. If this is happening it may be because their job prospects are

good, but it may also be that the organization still has a white, male ethos that marginalizes them. 'Exit interviews' may offer pointers for change.
24. In a redundancy situation, 'last in first out' will probably constitute indirect discrimination, as will a policy of first shedding part-time workers.

Conclusions

A housing organization that is truly serious about equal opportunities will first be aware of the range of target groups involved. Second it will consider carefully how to ensure that no group is subject to 'less favourable treatment' in service delivery over the full range of housing services, not simply those such as allocations where outcomes are relatively easy to investigate. A range of services could be subject to ethnic and other monitoring, but it must be remembered that monitoring itself does not constitute equal treatment but rather shows up the need for policy changes. Some issues of service delivery require not monitoring but an approach that recognizes individual differences: in particular design, whether of new homes, renovations or environmental improvements.

Equal opportunities policies are well-developed in a few authorities: unfortunately, they are often the very authorities under the greatest resource constraints. In most authorities and organizations the policies are minimal and their enforcement has low priority. One way to promote such issues in larger organizations is to have a specialized Women's Unit, Race Equality Team and Disabilities Unit. The organizational structure will depend on the scale of the organization. Such sections cannot be effective unless the section head has sufficient seniority and there is whole-hearted support at the political level (Stone, 1988). Any such unit should look at employment and service delivery issues, and should establish a working relationship with in-house trade unions.

No authority or organization can assume that equal opportunities policies have no relevance for them: very few have no ethnic minority population in their area and none is without women, disabled people or homosexuality — even if the latter is hidden. What more important role could a housing organization have than helping to create a community where everyone is respected and valued?

Acknowledgement

The author would like to thank Jenny Morris and Marion Roberts for their comments on a previous version of this chapter.

Part Two

Management Themes

4

Delivery of service

4.1 Introduction

The first part of the book examined the organization of housing services, the experience of decentralization and how equal opportunities should be considered and implemented. The next three chapters look at housing practice by means of case studies relating to certain themes, namely, delivery of service, homelessness and individual power and choice in the housing system. In each chapter the housing history of an individual is invented and the theme explored in relation to that history. This device means that certain omissions are necessary.

PROFILE A

Mrs Bunker's housing history is typical of many of her generation. She is 79 years old and is a widow. She moved to the Adelaide council housing estate at the time of her marriage, when she was 20 years old. She remained there for 55 years until her home became inconvenient and finally unmanageable.

The Adelaide estate, which was built in 1933, consists of 200 semi-detached, two and three bedroom houses situated on the edge of a medium-sized town. Over her lifetime the estate changed from a place where the early tenants were delighted with their homes and environment to an estate which was very unpopular. This gradual change was due to lack of investment in maintenance, unsuitable letting policies, vandalism and changing perceptions of good design.

Mrs Bunker lived in one of the three bedroom houses on a corner site with a large garden. During the latter part of her tenancy the house increasingly needed repairs and modernization but the response of the Council's maintenance service became worse. The reporting of repairs was made difficult by the abandonment of door-to-door rent collection. This difficulty was compounded by her deafness and dislike of using the telephone to report repairs. Such repairs as were carried out were often not done to her satisfaction, and rectifying them compounded the problems she faced.

In addition to the disrepair of the house, she was worried about the state of the garden which had become overgrown and encouraged visits from a variety of animals. The property and garden had been kept beautifully until her infirmities made bending and kneeling difficult. As a result of her increasing disability her social activities were curtailed and she was dependent on family and friends for help of all kinds. The location of the estate on the edge of town meant that the weekly shopping had to be done by neighbours although, in good weather, she managed to reach a local shop and post office. She was also dependent on neighbours to contact her family in an emergency. She found the stairs hard to manage and had ceased using the bath because of difficulties getting in and out of it.

At one stage her family had suggested that she move nearer to them, on the other side of town, but this was difficult as transfers and exchanges to their neighbourhood were rarely possible. As an independent-minded person she was not keen on the idea anyway, and wanted to move to sheltered housing. She saw such a move as giving her access to emergency help but being in her own self-contained home.

Having made the decision to move to sheltered housing Mrs Bunker placed her name on the transfer list for a home in a scheme near her relatives. Although the Council owned a number of sheltered housing schemes there was a considerable wait. She feared that the long wait might mean her health would have deteriorated to a point where she would have to go into a residential home. She was finally offered a home in a new scheme, reasonably near her relatives. In the interim, alternatives for keeping her in her home were discussed, but none suited her for financial and other reasons. These will also be considered in this chapter. A number of basic issues are raised by Mrs Bunker's situation and these will be discussed in sequence:

- the delivery of repairs and maintenance;
- the collection of rent and advice giving;
- the maintenance of the estate;
- the handling of complaints;
- the lettings system.

4.2 The basis of the relationship between landlord and tenant

An understanding of Mrs Bunker's position as a local authority tenant is first necessary. In any tenancy the basis of the landlord/tenant relationship affects the degree of comfort of the tenant. This is particularly true in the case of an elderly tenant like Mrs Bunker who is incapacitated.

The relationship between landlord and tenant is based on an agreement made between both parties. Prior to 1980 the terms set out were more than somewhat one-sided, with Councils including many petty rules and rarely listing their own obligations. The emphasis was on the tenant keeping the property in good repair and abiding by the rules. The Housing Act 1980 introduced a 'tenants' charter' which stimulated a re-writing of antiquated agreements and the provision of information to tenants. However, a Shelter survey in 1982/3 found that many authorities had not in fact issued information under s.44 of the Act as required. In these cases where re-writing had taken place the statutory repairing obligations of the council figured but not always comprehensively (Kay, Legg and Foot, undated). From anecdotal evidence the picture remains patchy.

On the tenants' side there is an obligation to use their home in a tenant-like manner and to carry out internal decorations. A model tenancy is outlined in Appendix A. The agreement can be fleshed out by a tenant's handbook detailing:

- access points for payment of rent;
- reporting of repairs;
- information on statutory services;
- fittings in the home and other local information.

It is important that such a handbook is 'tenant friendly', especially for people like Mrs Bunker. It should also be unpatronizing and written in clear English or other languages as necessary. It is worth noting that the new agreements have been ushered in alongside a debate about the necessity to remove the paternalistic image of council housing management (Clapham and English, 1987). Certainly the majority of tenants can manage their own affairs and expect efficient services in exchange for their rent, but a significant minority need more help, particularly in relation to money advice. A tenant like Mrs Bunker will need still other advice, for example on alternative housing options as she gets older.

The terms of an agreement on its own are not sufficient to guarantee a good relationship. The difference between the practices of authorities are highlighted in the Audit Commission Reports (1984 and 1986), leading to inequality of service in areas such as:

- seeking possession;
- chasing arrears;
- delivering a repair service;
- handling allocations.

Whilst the tone of an authority's management is set by its councillors and senior officers it is the frontline-staff who will have the onus of delivering.

The frontline-staff will bring their own perceptions and attitudes to their work, which will influence how they interact with tenants. Setting clear guidelines on attitudes and standards must be backed by training and support from senior management. Clapham and English (1987) suggest that 'the crisis in housing management is beginning to lead to a re-appraisal of its role and to attempts to change existing practices through local experiments'. There seem to be three different approaches in these 'experiments'.

1. The contractual nature of the landlord–tenant relationship is stressed and seeks to distance housing management from a social role.
2. The social role is embraced.
3. Control over housing management is devolved to the tenants themselves.

More often than not, all three approaches are used in the same housing organization. The contractual one for the bulk of tenants, the social role for the elderly and low income tenants like Mrs Bunker, and self-management where and when it is acceptable and viable. None of these approaches can be successful without a basis of good practice.

4.3 Service delivery

The basic services which Mrs Bunker and her neighbours required were as follows:

- a good repair and maintenance service;
- a well-tended estate;
- convenient methods of paying rent;
- advice and information on money matters;
- welfare services when needed.

The area office is the essential key to providing these services. In the next few sections the work of the area office in relation to Mrs Bunker's housing needs, will be examined after a brief comment on structures.

4.3.1 Structures

Unified function

Mrs Bunker had difficulty paying rent, obtaining repairs and information on alternative solutions to her housing situation. The best way to resolve such problems, and to deliver a good service generally, is by unifying the housing function, that is to provide a single point of contact for tenants for all housing services, with some means of communication to the housebound. This may be organized from a central office or in an area or neighbourhood office. The fragmentation of services referred to in Chapter 2, must be overcome, and this is more fully discussed in the Audit Commission Report (1986). There are other alternative structures which can be used for delivering the service, namely, Estate Management Boards and Tenant Management Co-operatives. Such structures would allow tenants more control over their housing, and are discussed more fully in Chapter 6. However, as already pointed out, it is not enough to have the right structure; it also is necessary to have committed staff of good quality, give opportunties for training and ensure that basic procedures and communication systems are clear and sensitive to tenants' needs. Efficient area office staff are also crucial to the smooth running of an office and as back-up to the estate staff.

The area office is increasingly being seen as the unit to deliver day-to-day management services. The prime services are:

• rent collection;
• delivery of repairs and maintenance;
• benefit advice;
• letting of properties.

Estate managers would be responsible for part of an area in a team managing from 3000 to 10 000 tenancies. The number of tenancies per staff member would vary according to the needs of an estate. For an estate such as Mrs Bunker's, one member of staff would be responsible for 300–500 properties. For a larger and more modern estate, a manager might have 1000 tenancies or more. A manager's responsibilities would include the following:

• collection of rents;
• giving benefit advice;
• settling neighbour disputes;
• liaising with tenants' groups;
• generally maintaining the estate and properties;
• arranging lettings;
• carrying out inspections to empty properties.

The office team would include:

• administrative staff;
• clerical staff;
• reception counter staff.

The administrative and clerical staff would deal with accounts, administer waiting lists, filing, typing, etc. The reception staff would deal directly with the public, receiving requests, complaints and queries. The housing team would also include:

- wardens of sheltered housing;
- caretakers;
- maintenance staff, who report to the area/neighbourhood office.

Figure 1.1, p. 17, shows the organization of a typical area (local) office.

4.3.2 Repairs and maintenance

As has been noted in Mrs Bunker's housing history, repairs and maintenance figured as a major problem. She had difficulty reporting repairs, getting them done and being satisfied by the result. The report by Stanforth *et al.* (1986) on the delivery of repair services in public sector housing in Scotland highlights many of the reasons for poor services which can be generally applied. These area as follows.

- The responsibility for repairs may be with more than one departmant. (The split is usually between the Housing Department and the Works Department.)
- The interpretation of who is liable for repairs is variable, and communication with tenants inadequate.
- There is a general lack of training of non-technical staff, who often are the people the public initially report to.
- Most of the authorities in the survey pre-inspected fewer than 40% of the repairs and post-inspection was less than 30%. In fact the tenant was the principal agent for quality control.
- Predicted response times varied considerably, an example being a defective immersion heater taking anything from 2 to 14 days to fix.
- A lack of planned maintenance.
- Inadequate records with a lack of a monitoring procedure for performance in financial and completion terms.

Many of these reasons were relevant to Mrs Bunker's disatisfaction with her home and her desire to move. The case studies in the survey (Stanforth *et al.*, 1986) highlighted her greatest complaint which was the delay in carrying out repairs and poorly executed work. Delays in repairing faulty front door locks or worn floorboards caused her to worry about the possibility of intruders and her physical safety. Her infirmities made communication with the local office difficult. Often the telephones were engaged or no-one answered. If she was able to speak to a member of staff, that person often had no direct knowledge of building construction. It was not easy, therefore, to deduce what work was necessary from the limited description given by Mrs Bunker. She was made dependent on visits from the housing staff or on friends/neighbours to report her repairs. Checking the completed work was also difficult for her unless it was an obvious repair like a dripping tap.

Some of Mrs Bunker's problems might have been made easier by organizational changes, which would have improved the service namely:

- putting the repairs service under one department;
- computerization of reporting and ordering repairs.

The arguments as to whether the service is best under one department is not resolved by the Scottish survey. The authority which scored highest on satisfaction had the responsibilities split between two departments but it also used contractors rather than the Direct Labour Organization (DLO). If the service is efficient then the split is immaterial, but inefficiency means that the housing management department bears the brunt of complaints from tenants and has no control over the outcome. The greatest risk which arises when more than one department is involved is in the loss of reports, orders, etc., and disputes over responsibility. A typical reporting system for two departments is listed in Appendix B. It is now a requirement under the Local Government Planning and Land Act 1980s 16(1) that the DLO makes a profit. In some authorities the DLO has become an efficient unit with locally-based repair teams with the Housing Department and Works Department co-operating. Such methods have proved 'highly popular, efficient and cost-effective' (Power, 1987).

The computerization of reporting and ordering of repairs can overcome, to some extent, problems like Mrs Bunker's non-technical description of a repair. It can also reduce the passing on of inadequate technical and general information from Housing to Works Department. Computer packages are available which have a step-by-step process leading non-technical staff through a series of questions relating to specific trades and defects. Questions are put to tenants in non-technical language which is a much easier process for a person like Mrs Bunker. An order is then transmitted to the appropriate trade gang or may be linked into a contractors' list showing which firm is available for work, thereby making best use of resources and time. Analysis of outstanding jobs, jobs completed and extracting trends are made easier and can lay the foundation for cost stations aimed at estate level. Such a system has been run by Bath City Council for some years and allow the non-technical staff member to be placed in either a Works department or a local housing office (Kirkwood, 1984).

The recommendations of the survey by Stanforth *et al.* (1986) and the Association of Metropolitan Authorities' good practice guide (1988) summarize what is good practice. The most important of these are as follows.

- Tenants should be given a much clearer idea about what their responsibilities are and how the repairs service operates.
- Tenants' groups should be involved in the monitoring of performance and in the introduction of any changes (Housing Act, 1980 s.43 requires this).
- Regular staff training should be given a high priority.

- Authorities should aim at all repairs being completed in 4 weeks.
- Tenants should be given a clear idea of when access is required.
- Higher levels of post-inspections are necessary to improve quality control. Tenants should be asked to check routine repairs and formally indicate their satisfaction or disatisfaction.
- Repair records should be improved and a data base for all properties instituted.
- Performance should be monitored with computers being used to a greater extent.
- Encourage residents to undertake small repairs and reward with a cash bonus. (Under common law residents have a right to use rent for this purpose.)
- Authorities should decentralize and the DLO should be locally based, with departments ensuring co-ordination. Wherever possible DLO and contractors should be used interchangeably to give greater flexibility.

These recommendations would improve the service for all tenants, but elderly tenants have particular needs. Other recommendations should have been made which are relevant to the infirmities and worries of old age, such as the following.

- Information concerning the impaired hearing of many elderly people should be passed on to the trades people.
- Instructions should be given to clear up after a job. A 79 year old may have difficulty in clearing up carpentry chippings.
- Workers should always have and show an identification card, but this system should be supplemented by advance notice to blind tenants.
- Tenants with impaired sight should receive help to identify repairs and subsequent checking on completion.
- A translation service should be available for those tenants whose English is poor or non-existent.
- There should be regular training for maintenance staff to enhance an awareness of these requirements and engender a helpful and understanding attitude.

It is imperative to have targets in mind, towards which an organization works. The implications of these improvements for the cost of the service is an important issue, but will not be discussed here. Not making changes can be as costly as leaving well alone. No organization can afford to leave its capital assets steadily declining.

4.3.3 The estate manager's work

In addition to the ordering and checking of repairs within a system such as that discussed in the previous section, the estate manager's other tasks

(p. 71) will be briefly discussed under the headings of rent collection and advice giving, sundry management and lettings.

Rent collection and advice giving

From the point of view of an authority, an effective rent service can reduce management costs, improve cash flow and landlord/tenant relations. It was suggested by the Audit Commission (1984) that to provide the best type of rent service a number of principles should be followed:

* rent accounting concentrated in the housing department;
* an estate manager responsible for a patch in a decentralized or area base system;
* tenants should know where they stand (an up-to-date rent card or regular statement);
* authorities must demonstrate that they are prepared to take prompt action to recover debt;
* have good control over void properties to ensure rent is not lost;
* possibly to give incentives to encourage regular payment, e.g. rent-free weeks.

A further principle should be the establishment of a variety of convenient contact points for payment of rent, and where necessary individual collection of rent from elderly or disabled people who request it. Mrs Bunker experienced a problem in paying her rent, which primarily stemmed from the withdrawal of the door-to-door rent collection service. The alternatives open to her were to pay by:

* bank transmission;
* giro method;
* payment direct to a housing office;
* Western Union shop points.

The last two methods were closed to her because of her inability to get out and about. Bank transmission was not possible as she did not have a bank account, which many pensioners do not. Giro had been possible but the authority decided to discontinue its use because of cost to the authority. She became, therefore, dependent on friends and neighbours paying at the office or sending money through the post. On occasions entries were incorrectly recorded, leading to misunderstandings between Mrs Bunker and her friends or neighbours and the Council. Because she received a small pension of £2000 per annum from her husband's occupational pension, she was just on the limit of income support. She occasionally fell into arrears, so that the accuracy of recording the amount paid and the amount shown in advance or arrear was very important. Generally pensioners are less likely to fall into arrears because:

- their income does not fluctuate too much;
- they often receive benefit;
- they are more experienced in managing a household budget.

At a certain income level Mrs Bunker could have become eligible for housing benefit. At this stage she would have been in need of advice and help to complete forms and get explanations about changes. Estate Managers need to have a good working knowledge of the benefit system so that they are able to judge the possible outcome of a benefit application. Handheld computers like BENE and FERRET can be purchased, which will operate up-to-date packages of benefit calculations making this aspect of advice giving easier. In 1989/90 explanations of the changeover from Rates to Community Charge and Water Rate changes have also been necessary and have taken up a high percentage of staff time.

The introduction of the charge has also affected the payment of housing benefit, causing widespread delays. This has led to increasing debts for numbers of people. On occasions people who have never previously been in debt have been caught in the system and experienced unnecessary worry. The situation can be aggravated by the immediate activation of standard debt recovery procedures, which do not always include the flexibility of an early visit. A typical good procedure involves the following:

- a written reminder/visit after 2 week's rent has been missed;
- a visit after 3 weeks and a negotiated weekly payment in addition to the weekly rent;
- a warning letter if the bargain is broken;
- at a fixed sum, a warning letter that a notice for seeking possession will be served;
- service of a notice for seeking possession;
- court proceedings to gain a suspended notice for possession;
- eviction after returning to the Court for permission to execute the notice.

Where elderly persons are concerned visits and explanations are doubly important. It is a fine judgement on what action to take and when. The estate manager is a pivotal point in operating these procedures and interpersonal skills. However, the manager has to take account of the landlord's requirements as well as those of the tenants. The principles stated by the Audit Commission give a reasonable framework within which to operate. Clearly-written procedures on debt recovery known to staff and tenants can ensure that unreasonable and illegal steps cannot be taken. Incentives to pay regularly are welcome to tenants. Lastly the control of empty properties not only reduces rent loss but demonstrates good management to the tenants. Despite following these good practice principles, there will always be a hard core of debtors for a variety of reasons. A policy decision will be needed on how much debt can be carried.

Nationally, the level of debt is causing concern. Recently the debt has increased because of rent rises and cuts and alterations to housing benefit. The national debt at the end of 1989 was £450 million pounds (Audit Commission, 1989). Reasons for tenant debt are various and not always due to an unwillingness to pay. Research by Duncan and Kirby (1983) suggests that low income is the primary cause, and that the most likely people to fall into arrears are large families, single parent families or those with pre-school or school age children. A sudden disaster, like unemployment or serious illness may also affect the ability to pay. A heavy concentration of debtors in Inner London and ten housing authorities outside London account for almost 50% of the total arrears (Audit Commission, 1984). To contain arrears, it is necessary to have accurate and up-to-date information on rent accounts coupled with clear procedures for contacting and advising tenants as early as possible after running into debt. Tenants should also be clear on the consequences of not paying.

Information on non-payment can be relayed in the Tenants' Handbook and Newsletters.

Sundry management

Three areas are chosen for comment, maintaining the estate, dealing with tenant's complaints and liaison with tenant groups. Mrs Bunker will have made use of or experienced these services at some time whilst living on the Adelaide estate.

Maintaining the estate

The poor environment of the Adelaide estate was a reason for the gradual increase in difficulty of re-letting homes. Vacant pieces of land were strewn with rubbish, empty properties were vandalized, street lighting was inadequate and too many dogs roamed the streets. Mrs Bunker's unkempt garden contributed to the general decline, through no fault of her own. Her feelings of insecurity were deepened by the changes she saw happening. It is the job of the estate manager to ensure that these problems are solved. It may be through liaison with the Works or Parks departments or it may be by supervising a caretaker/maintenance worker. A number of improvement initiatives have been tried by various authorities like PEP, and The Safe Neighbourhood Unit projects (Bright and Petterson, 1984). Beat-policing has become fashionable again and can help with curtailing vandalism and petty crime (NACRO, 1988). To keep a high standard, it is necessary to remove evidence of vandalism, replace lights as soon as possible and maintain regular cleaning cycles.

Dealing with complaints

Most tenants complaints arise from a poor repair and maintenance service or the look of the estate. Good organization can limit these. However, disputes occurring between neighbours are usually the more difficult to deal with. Mrs Bunker's disputes were with neighbours complaining about the state of her garden.

Management policies vary between a non-interventionist approach and to one where a manager will take some steps to resolve a difficulty. In the case in point only outside help could solve the problem, so understanding was required on the part of the neighbour. In some cases a Council will arrange for a volunteer group to tidy gardens or pay someone to do it. Complaints like a loud and late party or dog nuisance can be dealt with under the terms of the tenancy agreement. Where the dispute is one of personality and temperament between neighbours, a manager's skill in persuasion or mediation is called for. Ultimately the matter may have to be resolved by civil action between the neighbours in the court.

Liaison with groups

Part of the manager's role is to work with tenants' associations or groups. These may be groups which come into being in answer to a grievance or be deliberately fostered by the authority and have formal elections. They may be used to help to overcome some neighbour disputes, but are more likely to be used in a consultative capacity in modernization or improvement schemes. In such an instance the estate manager liaises between authority and groups. The groups will often liaise with individual tenants, a practice of value to elderly tenants. There is further discussion of this role in Chapter 6.

Lettings

In a large area office the decision as to who will be offered a tenancy lies with the lettings staff. The general policy framework is set by the Housing Committee. A waiting list of applicants and tenants wishing for transfer is compiled, often on a joint pointing basis, to ensure equality between applicant and tenant. The following is a typical procedure which Mrs Bunker would have had to follow to obtain a transfer.

- She would have asked the estate manager for a transfer form and had discussions on the chances of a move.
- The form would be completed and passed to the lettings officer.
- The lettings officer would have checked the data on types of property, availability and location and tried to match her request.
- The estate manager may also have culled the list and made suggestions to the lettings officer.
- She would have been notified when a suitable move became vacant.
- A direct exchange of properties may have been suggested.

The matching of households to homes and administering the waiting list is a difficult task but has been made somewhat easier by the introduction of computer programs. Details can be entered and easily recalled, matched and cross-referenced. Once an applicant or tenant has been offered a home and accepted, an agreement will be typed by clerical staff, ready for signing. This is the end of the lettings task and the file is passed to the appropriate estate manager.

This thumbnail sketch of the work of an estate office can only give a flavour of the variety of jobs undertaken. A tenant like Mrs Bunker should be able to:

- feel confident that a telephone call to the office or a request for a visit will be handled swiftly;
- receive understanding of the difficulties of elderly tenants and a time allowance made for her.

4.4 Problems and solutions for the elderly

There will inevitably be increasing numbers of tenants of pensionable age and thought should be given to an improved housing service for them. Given a good service and choice of property there will be less reason for people to move. However, Mrs Bunker's housing profile suggests good reasons for wishing to leave her three-bedroom house. Like many people over 75 years old (an arbitrary figure for some people are vigorous at that age) she finds the garden too big, the stairs and bathing difficult, is dependent on others for shopping, pension collection, etc., is lonely and worries what will happen in an emergency. She may be forced to remain in inappropriate property because of inflexibility in the stock, and the lack of income to move to another tenure.

In offering solutions to older people the paramount objective must be to locate the solution most appropriate for the person concerned in social and financial terms (Williams, 1986). Mrs Bunker's preferred option was to move to sheltered housing although other options were available to her. Those options that are available to her are explored in the next few sections.

Mrs Bunker's preferred choice to move to rented sheltered housing is popular with a number of older people. Sometimes this is chosen because there is no other alternative available. Approximately 6% of elderly people occupy this type of housing, provided by both local authorities and housing associations. Usually they must be of pensionable age although the age may be lowered for reasons of disability. Schemes consist of a development of flats or bungalows linked to a warden by a communication/alarm system. The warden's role is to act as a good neighbour and it follows that tenants should be reasonably independent. Obviously as time passes tenants will become more frail and need more support; ultimately some will have to move to residential homes or hospital. To take account of this, housing developments have incorporated residential homes where tenants can move on but remain in the same area as their friends. Others have converted present schemes to increased support in the form of meals provision and care attendants who will help with domestic and personal tasks. These 'very sheltered' or 'extra care' housing schemes are a means to continue independence, leaving residential homes for those who need 24 hour nursing. These schemes will be discussed later.

4.4.1 Management of sheltered housing

For Mrs Bunker the major attraction of sheltered housing is the presence of the warden who acts as an emergency helper and as the means of communication, when necessary, to relatives, friends, doctors and statutory helpers. Her experience in her home had led to isolation and a feeling of insecurity. She was lucky to enter Burns House, where the warden had a kindly disposition, a fund of common sense and had received proper training. At 75 years, Mrs Bunker joined a group of people spanning an age range from 60 to 90 years plus, from a variety of backgrounds and with differing expectations. Meeting their needs is a demanding task. The recently-developed Warden's certificate has enhanced the warden's status and shows how much skill, commitment and know-how is required (Job description, Appendix C). It is a demanding task not only for the warden but also for the local management back-up, and this has not always been recognized. Estate managment staff need to support the warden, ensuring good relations with the medical and social work departments. At some stage, some tenants will pass the point of the warden's help. It may then be necessary to make a joint management decision drawing in the tenant, their family and medical practitioner, as to when and where they move on to a hospital or residential home. Mental confusion and loss of control of bodily functions are the main reasons for having to move.

The management of sheltered housing is time consuming for estate management staff. Mrs Bunker required the following:

1. a visit to assess her housing need;
2. a visit to show her the plans and offer her a choice of flat;
3. a visit to show her the scheme on completion;
4. liaison with social services on any necessary adaptations;
5. one or two re-assurance visits;
6. liaison with her family on removal dates;
7. signing up the tenancy and handing over the keys;
8. liaison with the new warden about removal dates, names of nearest relatives and medical practitioners, and information on the working of equipment in the new flat;

9. keep an eye on the scheme on removal day;
10. a check that she had settled in and explanation of the flat's equipment, method of paying rent, reporting repairs, etc.;
11. an explanation of the alarm system (this would be reinforced by the warden);
12. advice giving on the benefit system;
13. a check on the sheltered building after 6 months to ensure that there are no outstanding minor repairs which are the responsibility of the builder;
14. regular visits to check on the running of the scheme.

Research has shown that a move at Mrs Bunker's age can prolong the life of most movers, but on occasion the upheaval may cause premature death (p. 000). Therefore time taken to reduce the worry of moving is well spent.

In Mrs Bunker's case, after the settling down period had elapsed, all building snags were eliminated. Social events were initiated and the use of the communal sitting room and kitchen were extended to the surrounding community. This led to a widening of Mrs Bunker's circle of friends, and she settled into her new life. The development of the social life of the sheltered housing scheme was enhanced by the work of the warden who sought to welcome new activities and uses in the communal room. The guest room was also well used and Mrs Bunker's old friends from further afield could stay.

At the end of the first year the tenants were asked for their views on:

- the running of the scheme;
- the warden's work;
- the design of the scheme;
- heating efficiency;
- general comments.

This feedack is useful information on which to assess the success of the warden's attitudes and workload as well as the tenants' comfort. Their views coincided with what is on the whole a general viewpoint, that there is great satisfaction with this type of housing (Butler, Oldham and Greve, 1983). The reassurance of having a person to call on in an emergency gives peace of mind which is reflected in better health. There is also the companionship of others, if desired, through use of the common room. However, there are drawbacks such as disruptions caused by the onset of senility in others, a person wandering into the wrong flat or imaginary persecutions — all these can be very upsetting to others.

4.4.2 Frail elderly schemes

At some future time Mrs Bunker may need more care and help than the warden can give. By increasing the standards of care and help in a scheme, it is possible for tenants to remain with friends and in familiar surroundings.

Schemes for the frail elderly involve extra care, which has been defined broadly as involving help with all or any of the following tasks:

- dressing;
- use of toilet;
- bathing;
- mobility;
- getting in and out of bed;
- grooming;
- eating.

Less personal tasks may include: housekeeping and personal affairs, laundry, shopping and giving of medication (NFHA, 1986a). Guidance has also been produced by the Housing Corporation (circular HC02/85). These schemes have become known as category two-and-a-half schemes, because they add on a care element to the sheltered housing standards of the Category 1 and 2 schemes originally laid down in DOE Circular 82/69. They were developed by, amongst others, Servite Housing Association and Richmond Churches Housing Trust as part of a pilot programme proposed by the National Federation of Housing Associations to cater for the increasing numbers of frail elderly. A scheme provided by the Guinness Trust includes hairdressing facilities, a luncheon club, a day centre staffed by Newham Council and a chiropody service run by the Health Authority which has been extended into a clinic for the area (Hunt, 1986).

Carers

With such a small percentage of older people housed in sheltered housing it is obvious that a great number are looked after by their families or struggling on their own. Of those cared for by families a significant number have single carers, often of pensionable age themselves. A study of informal carers on behalf of DHSS as part of the 1985 General Household Survey, showed that about 6 million people (14% of the adult population over 16 years) provide a regular service for someone who is sick, elderly or handicapped (Green, 1985). An interesting development by Sanctuary Housing Association with the National Council for Carers and their elderly dependents (NCCED) is described by Green. A supportive sheltered environment has been created with an emergency help system which is being upgraded to a 24 hour system. The carers are resident and continue to give the health care to their relatives but they also have access to the statutory services, and can receive a break from care and do not have the total burden of care. Sharing experiences with other carers is of itself a safety valve.

The estate manager's job in this area is primarily to:

- ensure the smooth running of the scheme;
- help to select the wardens, nurses, cleaners and care attendants;
- liaise with outside bodies such as NCCED, the health authorities and DSS;
- maintain the property.

All such schemes as these are in some jeopardy with the changes in benefit rates (NFHA, 1989) and the cuts in resources to authorities and the Housing Corporation. The advent of community care policies will also affect the way in which schemes are operated in future, as authorities will be expected to act as enablers and buy services for those in need of extra care (Cmnd. 849, 1989).

There is no doubt that sheltered housing and extra-care schemes fulfil an important need. However, there are many people who wish to remain in their own homes and who could be made comfortable or given extra help to enable them to do so. The alternatives which might have been chosen by Mrs Bunker are now considered.

4.4.3 Modernization

The houses on the cottage estates of the 1930s were relatively spacious although badly arranged by present day standards. In a study in 1982 it was found that six out of ten respondents wished to move. Disatisfaction with the property was related to the size and the 'need for maintenance and repairs, sometimes including modernisation of bathrooms and replacement of window frames' (Rose, 1982). Modernization is a great inconvenience even in the short-term and a stressful time for tenants. It may also bring special risks to the elderly. For example, the City University research (1978) reported that an old man died of cold because he considered that the costs of using the offered electric fire were too great.

The decision whether to modernize whilst tenants are in residence or move them out is a major issue. There is an advantage to the authority to work around the tenant in terms of cost and policing the work. However, many tenants would prefer to move to temporary housing and return on completion of the modernization. Authorities have approached the problem in a variety of ways. Three examples are described, none of which, however, would have been a solution to Mrs Bunker's problems. Some methods could have solved her internal house problems but not the sense of isolation, insecurity and the maintenance of her garden.

Example 1

The introduction of a limited package of improvements, to be carried out with the tenant in residence and within a set period of time by a specialist contractor.

The GLC used a 4 day package in which the bathroom and kitchen were re-planned and re-fitted, with a gas-fired central heating and hot water system being installed at the same time. Specialist contractors were employed who became:

- adept at keeping to the time schedule;
- liaising with tenants and the modernization officer;
- ensuring sub-contractors carried out their work;
- clearing up after the work was done.

This sounds ideal but evidence from the City University research (1978) suggests that what happens more often is slippage of all sorts. These include:

- tenants not being consulted prior to the programme;
- failure to carry out a programme of repairs beforehand leading to considerable delays in certain houses;
- lack of liaison between tenant, modernization officer and the contractor, upsetting phasing of the work and the temporary removal arrangements (decanting);
- sub-contractors not sticking to schedules;
- tenants not told when workers were arriving;
- weather delays which may shoot a contract over into the next financial year. This highlights the crazy system of annual budgeting.

These criticisms still hold good and pose problems for elderly tenants. Mrs Bunker only wished for small improvements, and it is open to argument whether it is reasonable to insist on large scale change in her house. A chair lift on the stairs or the installation of an internal WC and shower unit would have solved her internal house problems.

Example 2

Offering a package of improvements similar to Example 1, but housing the tenants in mobile homes and completing in a 2 week period.

Tameside MDC and a local contractor arranged such a programme and delivered the improvements with the minimum disruption. Such a method eliminates some of the problems listed above, but does nothing for Mrs Bunker's personal problems. Indeed it adds to them by this unpheaval of leaving her home.

The final example is a rather better option to solve her internal house problems but still leaving her with her social ones.

Example 3

Experiments with giving tenants choice from a limited number of improvements, or within cash limits or via the grant system.

This alternative to dictating what is to be modernized has been tried by Glasgow, Sheffield, and Hammersmith in London. Glasgow experimented with giving tenants a set sum which could be used on a menu of improvements with reasonable success. Sheffield used the discretionary power to make grants available to public sector tenants (Sharp, 1987); an option no longer open under the new grant regulations. There may be a case for using the minor grant assistance scheme for work for elderly tenants on benefit (Local Government and Housing Act, 1989). Hammersmith have a scheme whereby tenants can spend a number of points which relate to a variety of improvements and an increase in rent, thus allowing tenants considerable choice.

A series of case studies in 'New Homes from Old' (DOE, 1985) describes schemes carried out by authorities in partnership with developers, and highlights the problems for all participants. Whatever the system used modernization has to be sensitively introduced and carried out when elderly people are involved.

4.4.4 Alarm systems

A solution which might have overcome Mrs Bunker's social problems but not her housing ones is that of a personal or communal alarm system. Since the 1960s there has been a growing interest in the provision of alarm systems which provide an emergency call service. These may take the form of personal alarms of which there are a great variety on the market, or a central alarm system run by a local authority or housing association. Users of the latter system are linked by telephone to a central control unit where staff take messages and relay them to the caller's nearest relative, doctor or send a peripatetic warden to help. Initially, local authorities provided the service to enable their own elderly tenants to be linked in to local sheltered schemes. The building of sheltered housing has become increasingly expensive and the provision of community alarm systems is seen as a cheaper method of providing the emergency contact (Tinker, 1984).

The service can be extended to owners, housing association and private tenants. The weekly cost of an alarm for housing association tenants is eligible for housing benefit if the housing has been specifically adapted or designed for elderly persons. Private sector owners or tenants are not eligible although local DSS offices have discretion to pay.

There is a danger that this technological solution may be seen as a simple answer to older peoples' problems (Fisk, 1984). It should not be a substitute for good care-and-support solutions or human contact. In Mrs Bunker's situation an alarm system might have overcome her sense of insecurity but not her physical isolation. An example of such a broader service is 'Rothercare' the system set up by Rotherham MDC. The central unit is capable of serving thousands of users and a start has been made with connecting local housing associations. Feedback from an investigation of tenant satisfaction with Rothercare, carried out by Sheffield degree students (1986) showed that tenants greatly appreciate the peace of mind it gives, but figures of its use do not suggest, however, that the cost of the system is justifiable. It is difficult to feed into the assessment how much money may have been saved by the service allowing people to stay in the own homes, and thereby enhancing the quality of their lives. Such objectives should after all be important in any public service.

4.4.5 Adaptations

The OPCS disability surveys (1988) indicate that a large proportion of the six million adults in Britain having some physical, mental or sensory disability are over 65 years old. The disabilities range from slight to severe. Mrs Bunker who has difficulty with stairs and getting in and out of the bath is one of many in a similar predicament. The provision of suitable aids or adaptations could allow her to remain in her home and this work can be carried out by the local authority. The key people to approach to obtain help are the doctor and the occupational therapy sevice of the social services. The type of adaptations available are as follows:

- grab rails for the bath;
- extra handrail on the stairs;
- widened doorways for wheelchairs;
- toilet/shower downstairs;
- stairlift.

There is also a variety of equipment such as walking frames and high-seat chairs available. Ideally more new and rehabilitated homes should be provided to mobility standard (DOE, 1975). The doctor is the passport to a number of health-related services such as home helps, meals on wheels, day care, short stay care and welfare benefits such as attendance allowances (Goslyn, 1988).

The provision of appropriate adaptations or equipment, allied to use of the central alarm system and domiciliary help, could result in many older citizens remaining in familiar surroundings and prolonging their lives. Sadly, political commitment to the financing of such services is not high.

4.4.6 Sheltered housing for sale

As Mrs Bunker had to experience a long wait for a transfer, she might have been able to exercise her right to buy and take advantage of the new option of 'sheltered housing for sale'. An owner sells their home and buys into a sheltered ownership scheme. Most schemes tend to cater for the better-off elderly, but theoretically Mrs Bunker could buy her home with the maximum discount and have sufficient capital to part-buy a sheltered home.

Full purchase is probably out of the question in a time of high house prices and interest rates. It might be made possible by an interest-only mortgage, but there are many pitfalls in this option. The economics of any transaction will vary in different parts of the country, and there are different types of schemes offering different amounts of equity.

Buying into a sheltered scheme may be accomplished in the following three ways.

1. By outright purchase of a property, usually provided by a private developer but managed by a Housing Association. On occasion the developer has a separate management company.
2. By buying 70% of the equity in a property and paying 30% in the form of rent. The rental element is eligible for housing benefit. These are known as Leasehold Schemes for the Elderly (LSE) and are provided both by housing associations and local authorities. It is a means whereby elderly owners whose homes do not raise sufficient capital to buy a property outright can gain access to some form of sheltered housing.
3. Shared Equity sale, similar to LSE but with varying purchase percentages.

The availability of these schemes will depend on different variables. In the case of private development, whether outright purchase or shared equity, it will be house prices and profit margins. LSE and Equity sales schemes may be dependent on Housing Corporation monies in the form of Housing Assocation Grant or private funding which will raise the level of the rental element. A further concern is the spiralling of service charges of purchased sheltered housing for many elderly people who are on a fixed income. An additional worry to buyers can be a clause in the purchase agreement stipulating that the purchaser must move out if they can no longer look after themselves. Some big schemes overcome this by providing residential move-on housing. Research by Butler *et al.* (1983) showed that 50% of tenants in sheltered housing leave for reasons other than death. The staging post of 'extra-care housing' discussed earlier is, therefore, increasingly a necessity. Of these three schemes only the Equity Sharing would be possible at 1990 prices for most elderly owners. For Mrs Bunker even this option is not financially viable as she has insufficient income to buy her council home under the right to buy regulations.

4.4.7 Staying put or care and repair

One other alternative would be open to Mrs Bunker if she exercised her right to buy and then found at a later date that substantial repairs were needed.

That option is the 'Staying Put' or 'Care and Repair' schemes. 'Staying Put' was pioneered by the Anchor Housing Association as a means to help low income pensioners release capital on their homes in order to carry out repairs, adaptations, etc. The parallel scheme 'Care and Repair' grew out of the Ferndale project in the Rhondda Valley and has been promoted by Shelter, the National Campaign for the Homeless and the Housing Associations Charitable Trust (HACT) (Morton, 1982). It has now been backed by the Department of the Environment, which in 1986 provided funds for Care and Repair Ltd to set up 25 new schemes in England by the end of 1988, on a matching fund basis. Five of these are to be set up by Anchor Housing Association. In December 1986 the Welsh office provided funding on the same basis to set up six schemes in Wales.

The schemes are designed to provide assistance to elderly home owners who would otherwise be unable to cope with keeping their homes in good order. Use is made of local authority grants, building society and other loans, and help from the DSS. Schemes combine the provision of advice with practical assistance and building work which may, in some circumstances, involve the use of direct labour at a low or subsidized cost. Evaluation of the 'Staying Put' schemes by Rose Wheeler (1985) shows that this initiative is a useful way of maintaining people in their own homes.

Conclusions

The range of options considered in this chapter should have been discussed with Mrs Bunker, even though her choice was sheltered housing. With the high cost of provision for this type of housing, organizations are likely to reduce the numbers of schemes, and elderly tenants will be forced to consider alternatives. No doubt she also thought that a move to sheltered housing would be her last move, but there is evidence to suggest that a significant number of people have to move to residential homes as frailty increases. Such homes may be provided by local authorities or private sector sources. Private sector provision of residential homes has snowballed, but they are not always of good quality and there is a lack of an adequate inspectorate. Housing Associations have started to enter the field of residential provision via frail elderly schemes and managing Homes transferred from the authorities. In the latter case, the associations will look after the property and the personal services will be provided by the social services department. Central government has spoken with two voices reducing investment in housing and at the same time given a clarion call for community care initiatives to be developed. The next few years will see major changes in this area.

It would seem, however, that suitable special housing for the elderly will be insufficient to meet the needs of the ageing population. The most sensible alternative to sheltered housing is to make Mrs Bunker as comfortable as possible in her own home. This will be a growing option with the installation of city-wide alarm systems which provide the emergency help and reassurance element. It will be necessary to ensure that home helps are available and that human contact is maintained. However, local authorities have to weigh up their obligations to all tenants and to applicants on the waiting list and might in consequence have wished to persuade her to move to a smaller home. Having spent 50 years in the same home this would have been an emotional wrench. A mutual exchange or transfer nearer her relatives would have presented the same problem. In any case her wish to remain independent demanded respect. The alternatives involving the right to buy as a first step proved financially unviable, as it will for many elderly tenants.

The increase in number of older people needing housing solutions to their social and physical problems presents a growing problem of co-ordination. This has led to a number of authorities appointing a policy advisor. The advisor is responsible for drawing up a strategic plan that co-ordinates resources, ensures information is issued and sets out the role of the authority in an enabling role. Such a role could not be put to better use than in the field of solving the housing problems of older people like Mrs Bunker.

5

Homelessness

5.1 Introduction

This chapter takes homelessness as its theme and profiles a young Afro-Carribean woman. Homelessness is not confined to the large cities and the difficulties encountered in the history are common to every part of the country.

First the statutory definition of homelessness will be examined, followed by the way the consequent tests for it are applied in practice. The attitudes of housing officers dealing with the homeless are critically reviewed along with the level of knowledge and the variety of structures with which they work. This section is rounded off by remarks on good practice for housing departments and on those areas, such as the Code of Guidance (1983)*, which still need clarification to ensure the homeless are treated sympathetically and fairly.

The chapter then moves on to review the housing alternatives open to the homeless, first noting the limitations on these alternatives imposed by the level of benefit payments. Accommodation of the homeless in Houses in Multiple Occupation (HMOs), Hostels, Short-life Housing and Womens' Refuges is reviewed in turn, noting particular situations regarding the management of hostels and short-life properties for housing departments. This section is completed by a review of the position on the vitally necessary 'move-on' housing, to get the homeless into permanent accommodation.

Finally, mention is made of the need for specialist support workers, and the chapter is illustrated throughout by reference to the case history.

PROFILE B

A 23 year old West Indian woman, Tracey Smith, left her home on a council estate at the age of 16 in 1982. The break came because of a disagree-

---

* A revised code of Guidance was issued in 1991. However the points made are relevant to the new guide.

ment with her parents over her lifestyle. She was able to live at a friend's home for a while, but when it became clear that she was not able to repair relations with her parents the friend's parents felt she should not stay any longer. She moved to a bed-and-breakfast hotel which she paid for, intitially, by benefit and then found a low-paid job. The job enabled her to move to a privately rented bed-sit flat in a HMO which she could only just pay for out of her earnings. After 12 months she lost the job, failed to pay her rent and in due course was evicted. Her local council did not consider her to be at risk and did not accept her as homeless. She lived rough for several weeks and finally found a service job in a hotel working as a chambermaid. This job gave her live-in-housing and food, plus a minimal wage. She found, however, that after a period of time the under-manager started to harass her verbally and physically. She complained about the under-manager but was not believed, and frightened of losing her job she was effectively coerced into having sexual relations with him, subsequently becoming pregnant by him. As a result of the pregnancy she was told to leave.

Again she had no alternative but to sleep rough and applied to the Council as a homeless person. She was judged not to be in priority need even though four months pregnant and just under 18 years old. Eventually she made friends with another woman and tried to find permanent housing. The only possibility was a short-life property in the ownership of a housing association, which the friends decided to rent. Friendship developed into a lesbian relationship which lasted 12 months. They then split up, with Tracey leaving the short-life property. After her previous experience at the Council she did not apply for acceptance as a homeless person. She was lucky enough to get into a short-stay hostel for young women, where she was allowed to keep the baby with her for a limited amount of time. This meant that she was driven into another venture into private renting which ended in eviction.

By now she had met a man with whom she developed a relationship and who had the tenancy of a local authority property. She obtained part-time work and lived for three years with her partner having a baby by him. Sadly the relationship became an increasingly violent one until she could no longer stand it. She left with the children and went to a womens' refuge in the area. Her partner found out where she was and harassed her there. She was moved to a refuge in another town where she was safe but away from her contacts and friends. The refuge workers helped her to approach the Council to gain priority status for permanent housing. The refuge was very crowded and after 6 months, as there was no offer from the Council, Tracey decided to try life with her partner again. For a period there was no violence but it inevitably re-started. She returned to the neighbouring town's refuge and this time remained. In the interval the local authority had made an arrangement to offer six properties a year to the refuge. So after a lengthy waiting time of two years Tracey received an

Table 5.1 Completions in all tenures in the United Kingdom, 1978 and 1988

United Kingdom	1978	1988
Public sector housing	136 437	33 505
Private sector	152 166	192 211
	278 603	225 716

Source: Housing and Contruction Statistics: Great Britain/DOE/SDD/WO. HMSO (1989).

offer of a two bedroom house in the town and gained a permanent home, albeit away from old friends and relatives.

5.2 Availability of stock

This is the crux of the matter. The number of homes being built and/or renovated are insufficient. The private rented sector has declined, owner occupation is being pushed to the limit and the new building programme has been reduced. In all the areas where the numbers of the homeless are growing, shortage of housing is the central problem. The evidence for this is the government's own figures in Table 5.1

Some local authorities keep a sort of programme going by partnership deals with building developers. The authorities either provide land at nil or low cost in exchange for homes being sold to waiting list clients or tenants, or sell off parts of an estate in exchange for demolition and rebuilding or refurbishing. In this way movement is occasionally maintained to release new lettings for the homeless. The capability of local authorities to provide permanent housing, therefore, is variable and depends on the number of acceptances of homeless people, the character of the stock and the turnover of lettings. The local authorities also nominate homeless people to housing associations.

5.3 Definition of homelessness

Tracey's search for housing foundered at the very start because of the law's exclusion of young single people unless considered vulnerable. A postal survey of all local authorities in England and Wales by Evans and Duncan (1988) showed that even where single people were of a vulnerable age, they would only be accepted in certain circumstances. Less than one in five authorities usually accepted them as vulnerable on the basis of age alone. There is every reason to believe that many people do not apply to councils assuming that it is futile to do so.

The law relating to homelessness is now contained in the Housing Act 1985 Part 111. Consolidated into this act is the Housing (Homeless Persons) Act 1977 containing the original homelessness legislation. There is also an amendment in the Housing and Planning Act 1986. The legislation was made necessary by the increase in the numbers of homeless people and the inadequacy of the response from the statutory agencies. Numerous charitable agencies working with homeless people brought pressure to bear on the government for some revision of the law. The reasons for this increase are complex but the major ones are:

- shortage of properties in the right places;
- demographic changes in society;
- expansion of ownership at the cost of rented properties;
- an increase in the formation of households through marital separation and young people leaving home at an earlier age.

The proposed definition of homelessness in the 1977 Act was broad but was watered down on its passage through Parliament. The present definition is based on three 'tests' against which authorities have to assess the circumstances of the people who present themselves as homeless. The questions which Tracey had to answer were:

- are you without satisfactory housing, or are you in imminent danger of losing your home?
- does your difficulty arise from circumstances beyond your control, or has it been brought about by your own action?
- do you fit within one of the following categories of 'priority need'? (families with young children, women expecting a baby, people vulnerable through old age, physical disability, mental handicap or illness).

Once these 'tests' were satisfied Tracey would have been entitled to assistance in securing a home. Her 'local connection' with an area would also have been checked to ensure that the particular authority was responsible for housing her.

The most controversial rule is that relating to 'intentional' homelessness. Essentially, if a person gives up housing which it would have been reasonable for them to continue living in or it was lost through their own fault they are considered to have become intentionally homeless. DOE (C of Guidance, 1983). However, if they were not aware of the relevant facts intentionality is not construed. Research carried out for the GLC by Bramley et al. (1988) showed that intentionality was found in only 1.6% of enquiries. This means that it is a rare occurrence or that the clause has acted as a 'deterrent which operates at an earlier stage in the process deterring potential claimants, especially when allied to the certainty of being given a period of temporary accommodation' (Bramley *et al.*, 1988). Tracey would not have been considered intentionally homeless.

The Code of Guidance states that the examination of what is intentional may go beyond the most recent accommodation to the last settled accommodation, which widens the scope of the clause. It spells out detailed circumstances where it is not reasonable to declare an applicant intentionally homeless but clarification is still needed on a number of points. For example, the position of people who move for employment purposes or find themselves homeless at the end of a holiday let or shorthold tenancy.

Research also suggests that, as with the 'intentional' clause, only a small number of people are unable to prove connection. Evans and Duncan (1988) found that one third of local authorities in their sample had no applicants at all in this category and on average other local authorities had only four. There is, however, a slightly higher number in non-Metropolitan boroughs and in Welsh authorities. There are guidelines in the form of the 'Local Authorities Association Agreement on Procedures for the Referral of the Homeless', which define residence as 6 of the previous 12 months, or 3 out of the previous 5 years. In addition employment is defined as not of a casual nature and family links should mean parents, adult children or brothers or sisters who have been resident at least 5 years. It is suggested by a report of the Institute of Housing (1988) that these guidelines be incorporated into the code of guidance. These rules apply equally to men with the obvious exception of pregnancy!

In 1989 the Secretary of State reviewed the legislation and re-affirmed the priority categories but decided to revise the Code of Guidance (DOE, 1989a), paying particular attention to 'local connection' and the use of 'bed-and-breakfast' (Dwelly, 1990). A re-definition of homelessness is still wished for by several bodies, some wishing to limit categories and others to broaden them. The argument is between a definition which says rooflessness only and a definition which takes acccount of people who are at risk of becoming homeless, for whatever reason, or who live in sub-standard conditions. The trend to broaden the definition for social and cultural reasons has been pursued by pressure groups such as Shelter and CHAR and has been accepted by the more liberal local authorities. It is best summarized in Bramley *et al.* (1988), that these people have in common 'the lack of a right or access to their own secure and minimally adequate housing space'. Sadly, 'realist' and 'minimalist' policies have been re-introduced because of the lack of a supply of homes' (Dibblin, 1989). In terms of the rules, on each occasion Tracey presented herself as homeless she should have been given priority status. On the first occasion she should have been considered at risk because of her age and vulnerability. On the second occasion the refusal to accept her was an incorrect interpretaton of the code. Her pregnancy should have placed her in a priority category. The codes of guidance issued by the DOE and Welsh

Office and the Scottish Office give clear and reasonably liberal guidelines on interpretion of the law. With regard to priority relating to pregnancy the wording is 'irrespective of the length of time they have been pregnant, and yet there is evidence from many sources* that this is ignored. Similarly on vulnerable young people 'Authorities should have particular regard to those who are vulnerable . . . to secure whenever possible that accommodation is available . . . for homeless young people who are at risk of sexual and financial exploitation'. This advice should have led to her being accepted as homeless. The central problem is the lack of a clear distinction between legal obligations and local authority discretion. This could be overcome by the Code of Guidance being clarified and made mandatory. The next section comments on the variety of interpretation and practice.

5.4 The variety of interpretation and practice

The lack of a standard interpretation of the homelessness legislation throughout the United Kingdom is due to a combination of the following.

1. The attitude and politics of councillors.
2. Professional attitudes, knowledge and structure.
3. Availability of stock.

It should be noted that legislation was introduced in England and Wales in 1977, in Scotland in 1978 and in Northern Ireland in 1988[†]. There is no difference in the legislation except that in Northern Ireland the Housing (NI) Order states that 'regard may be had, in determining whether it would be reasonable for a person to continue to occupy accommodation, to the general circumstances prevailing in relation to housing in Northern Ireland'.

5.4.1 Attitudes of councillors

Before local government re-organization in 1974, many local authorities were small, with councillors concerned with the detail of lettings and allocations. Authorities are now larger and policy making is much more complex. The accepted wisdom for many is that councillors set policy and officers execute

---

* Although most authorities will accept pregnant women as priority homeless, evidence of such is asked for and will vary from authority to authority. The studies in the text have evidence of this.

[†] Titles of the Homeless Acts are (a) Housing (Homeless Persons) Act 1977 which is now incorported into the Housing Act 1985 Part 111; (b) Homeless Persons Act (1977) Scotland; (c) Housing (NI) Act 1988.

it. However, in practice some councillors still take a close interest in detail and officers influence policy greatly.

The liberality of a policy will often depend on the background of the people concerned and the influence of national party attitudes. As a comment on the general attitudes of politicians to homelessness Pat Niner's research (1989) on the practice in nine local authorities suggests that 'the extent of homelessness, as measured by acceptances relative to council stock, was related to the general approach taken in a manner affected by political control. For a given pressure of homelessness, a more 'liberal' approach was associated with Labour control and a more 'strict' approach with Conservative control or a hung council following Conservative control'.

Local politicians also tend to take a narrow view of who should be housed, believing that local people should have first bite provided they deserve housing. They are also concerned with the possibility of queue jumping.

Abrahams & Mungall (1989) found that one of the determining factors for acceptance seemed likely to include 'the political and social attitudes of members and officers'. There is, however, evidence from the Audit Commission (1989a) that 'there is a wide overlap between people on the waiting list and the homeless'. Further evidence in Table 5.2 from the research by Bramley *et al.* (1988) into homelessness in London shows that people tend to have lived in the same district prior to seeking help. Tracey as a person not even on the waiting list would be regarded as a low priority for housing.

5.4.2 Professional attitudes, knowledge and structure

The most recent information on the working of the Homeless Sections is contained in the Audit Commission's report (1989), Niner's research (1989) and Evans and Duncan (1988). They reveal that a hard-pressed group of staff work with inadequate resources trying to help people in an increasingly desperate plight. The reports also reveal a wide range of methods, policies and attitudes for dealing with homelessness.

Attitudes

The attitudes of professional staff 'processing' the homeless are diverse. Evidence from Niner's (1989) research shows that most housing staff see themselves as being helpful and do not like having to ask the necessary personal questions to make the decision to accept people as homeless. However, quotations from applicants concerning the inquiries suggest that applicants see things differently.

> They wouldn't take my word for it that I was physically ill — so I had to get doctor's letters and hospital letters.

Table 5.2 Previous place of residence of homeless households (% of acceptances)

Previous residence	London					England				
	One month prior		One year prior			One month prior		One year prior		
	1975	1980	1980	1984	1985	1975	1980	1980	1984	1985
Same district/boro	91	90	79	74	78	92	90	81	84	86
Same county/London	inc UK	4	8	18	15		2	4		
Elsewhere in UK	7	2	6			6	5	9	12	11
Abroad	2	3	7	9	7	2	2	6	4	4

Source: Homelessness and the London Housing Market. Bramley *et al.* (1988). Occasional Paper 32.

I went to the woman with two black eyes and they asked if I had proof I'd been hit.

The antagonism generated is often difficult to deal with on both sides. Obviously authority staff have to verify certain facts, but their training and knowledge are not always sufficient. Applicants understandably become frustrated and upset. Apart from the general comments from a range of applicants there is also evidence from the Hackney Report (CRE, 1984) that leaves no doubt that a number of staff were racist in their approach to black applicants. More recently a report by staff of the Ealing Housing Aid Service (1986) covering an area with a high ethnic population states 'there is still evidence of a hostile approach to homeless people from certain officers and there is need for a written code of practice'.

In addition, Niner's research noted concern voiced by the staff of the Homeless Persons Units, that lettings and management staff might see the homeless 'as queue jumpers and potential problems who did not necessarily deserve priority' (Niner, 1989). This view parallels that of councillors in authorities who argue for a rigorous approach to acceptance of homeless people. This is a disturbing finding.

Knowledge

These staff attitudes are compounded by a lack of knowledge of the law and of the Code of Guidance, leading to the incorrect rejection of applicants like Tracey. The Audit Commission Report (1989) recommended that 'Written guidance for interviewing officers would help to ensure proper investigations and the exercise of the authority's discretion under the legislation in a consistent manner'.

The survey of authorities in the report showed that over 50% did not produce written guidance for staff. A further recommendation suggested that the local authority associations 'should consider the production of standard forms and guidance manuals at a national level in a format which could be adapted to local circumstances'. These should help to encourage consistency between authorities. Other research (Niner, 1989; Bramley et al., 1988) repeated the finding elsewhere that the whole homelessness process operated on the basis of the judgement of officers who were often on a fairly low grade. Tracey's housing chance depended on the level of knowledge of these staff. Such officers are often dependent for their knowledge on the informal discussions of the homeless team and occasional access to senior officers for consultation on particular aspects of the work, e.g. applying the intentionality clause. 'Few authorities had policies or procedure manuals and few had training programmes' (Niner, 1989).

Structure

The way in which departments structure their response to homelessness varies enormously. Some will have a single member of staff, others a section headed by a senior person who will supervise staff, write policy papers and have access to influential committees. In others the work is undertaken by departmental counter staff. Evans and Duncan's (1988) postal survey of local authorities reported that in England and Wales in 1986/87, out of an 89% response rate, 42% had specialist units, 11% specialist staff in housing advice centres or area offices and 52% incorporated homelessness duties into their general management duties. Figure 5.1 shows homelessness duties organized by authority. Such diversity of structures made Tracey's life difficult when dealing with different authorities.

Niner's research of nine authorities gives a cross-section of the structures in different sized authorities which will serve to make a number of points. In all case studies the chief housing officer had overall responsibility but the day-to-day work was carried out further down the line. Niner uses a useful simplification of the functions which homelessness officers have to carry out:

- initial interviewing;
- making enquiries and investigations;
- making decisions as to responsibility;
- arranging for temporary housing where needed;
- providing and managing temporary housing;
- providing permanent housing where appropriate;
- offering advice and assistance to the groups requiring it.

The organization of these functions in the case studies is shown in Table 5.3. As can be seen from the table there is wide variation in organization falling into four broad categories.

1. Specialized homeless person units dealing with all functions.
2. The service run from the housing advice centre, which was located away from the main housing department.
3. A decentralized housing service with neighbourhood offices where staff interviewed, investigated, decided on acceptance and provided advice and assistance when required. Alongside this a centralized unit deals with finding and managing temporary housing and acts as an information base for the neighbourhood staff.
4. The lettings section undertakes all homelessness duties as an integral part of its work.

The variety of structures and levels of responsibilities is striking and seems to be the outcome of responses to local conditions of numbers of enquiries and acceptances of homeless people and stock availability.

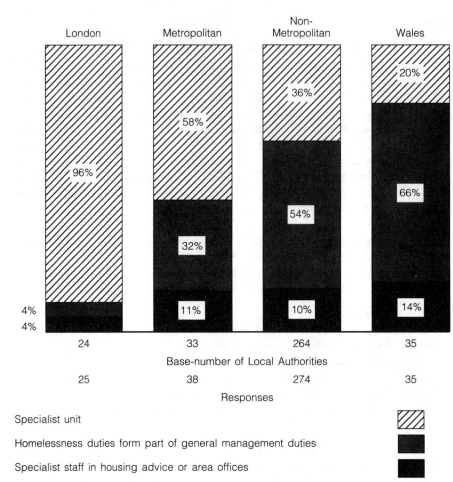

Figure 5.1 The organization of homelessness duties by type of authority.
Source: Evans and Duncan (1988) 'Responding to Homelessness'. Local authority policy and practice, DOE. Fig. 2 p. 7. With the permission of the Controller of HMSO.

5.5 Good practice and clarification of the Code of Guidance

5.5.1 Good practice

The perfect solution for Tracey would have been immediate permanent housing in an area of her choice, offered by staff who were understanding and efficient. The factors discussed in the previous section outline some of the reasons why this could not be accomplished. The task could have been ameliorated if good and consistent practice had been observed. To achieve

Table 5.3 Organization of the main homelessness functions

Authority	Interviews	Enquiries	Decision	Arrange TA	Manage TA	Permanent accom.	Advice
Type 1							
Cardiff	HPU	HPU	HPU	HPU	HPU	Lettings	HAC
Hillingdon	HPU/HAC	HPU	HPU	HPU	HPU	Lettings/area	HAC
Nottingham	HPU	HPU	HPU	HPU	HPU	Lettings/HPU	HPU
Westminster	HPU	HPU	HPU	HPU	HPU	Area letts/HPU	HPU
Type 2							
Gloucester	HAC	HAC	HAC	HAC	HAC	Lettings group	HAC
Newcastle	HAC	HAC	HAC	HAC	HAC	Estate officers	HAC
Type 3							
Birmingham	N'hood	N'hood	N'hood	Cent unit	Cent unit	N'hood	N'hood
Islington	N'hood	N'hood	N'hood	Cent unit	Cent unit	N'hood	N'hood
Type 4							
New Forest	Lettings	Lettings	Lettings	Lettings	Lett/Man	Lettings	Lettings

HPU   Housing Person Units
HAC   Housing Advisory Centre
N'hood   Offices in a decentralised service/central unit
Lettings   Section deals with all duties.
Source: From Niner (1989) 'Homelessness in nine local authorities: case studies of policy and practice' HMSO. With the permission of the Controller of HMSO.

this it is necessary to clarify aspects of the Code of Guidance and provide adequate staff and property resources. These matters will be discussed in the following section.

Tracey's initial interview was her first experience of a housing organization and held some terror of the unknown. Many people who have had bad experiences in bureaucratic situations will be surprisingly submissive and often inarticulate — an attitude born of despair. In some instances there is also difficulty with the language. Tracey was not knowledgeable about her rights and was in an overwrought state. A sensitive approach was therefore imperative. She was received by the regular management/counter staff in the housing department and interviewed to establish whether or not she could be considered for priority rehousing. The staff member was quite junior and lacked interview experience and proper knowledge of the law relating to homelessness. Greve's research (1986) comments on the lack of 'experience in the relevant areas of housing law and lack of "adequate training opportunities and facilities" by such members of staff dealing with homelessness'. Tracey was interviewed in a semi-private room where her conversation could be overheard. Research has shown (Niner, 1989) that waiting rooms 'were poorly or sparsely furnished and distinctly unwelcoming'. By contrast, Housing Advice Centres were generally better decorated, though space in all offices was at a premium and seemed to be 'affecting the efficient functioning of the unit'. Such settings are not a conducive atmosphere to calm clients who may be under threat of notice, already have a possession order against them, be in a refuge, squatting, or are threatened with violence. To be told at the end of an interview that they are not eligible for re-housing, or will have a long wait, increases their stress. It is vital, therefore, that good practice in meeting their needs is established.

The best existing practices may be distilled from the research by Niner (1989), Evans and Duncan (1988) and the Audit Commission (1989). The Institute of Housing has also made recommendations for future practice (1988); as has the Audit Commission's report (1989). These included the following.

- The present government's statistics relating to homelessness are inadequate. The Commission sees 'a case for establishing a standard model of data collection both for national statistics and for local management information'. This would enable the targeting of resources for temporary housing to the authorities with the greatest homelessness problems.
- Authorities should review the ratio of acceptances to the stock available and only accept people if there are sufficient permanent homes to offer them. It follows that there should be very clear policies for the exercise of the authority's discretion, for it means that an invidious choice has to be made between those in need and the very neediest.
- Those authorities with properties needing major repairs should be targeted

to receive resources. This would allow homes standing empty to be brought into use.

- There should be minimal use of temporary housing and it should be of a reasonable standard and good value for money.
- When authorities are forced to use bed-and-breakfast then the health, safety and comfort of the clients must be paramount.
- There must be maximum use of existing housing by raising the proportion of lettings offered to homeless clients, reducing the numbers of empty properties, aiming for a 3 week relet period outside London and 6 weeks in London.

It ducks the issue for London where some authorities are already letting to only homeless clients and cannot bring back properties into use because of lack of cash caused by reductions in central government funding.

All these recommendations of the Audit Commission are relevant to Tracey's experience in various forms of temporary housing. The Commission also recommended other ways of helping people like Tracey:

- giving cash grants to encourage existing tenants to buy in the private sector;
- creating tenancies by offering removal expenses to tenants of over-occupied homes to move;
- buying family-sized houses from elderly owners in exchange for a smaller home;
- making greater use of nominations and partnership schemes with housing associations;
- leasing arrangements with owners in the private sector;
- ensuring that empty homes in government departments like the Ministry of Defence, Health, etc., are made available to authorities and housing associations.

The success of these solutions is dependent on capital monies being available, with the exception of private leasing. The financial limitations placed on authorities and housing associations by central government allows only a small number of lettings to be created by such means. Private leasing has been used extensively in London (LRC, 1989), but the 6-year limit is short in comparison to the lead time necessary to get a building programme started. Overall it is clear that 'there is a strong case for taking greater account of homelessness in the allocation of capital resources by central government to local authorities' (AC, 1989).

5.5.2 Clarification of the Code of Guidance

Alongside the need for 'good practice' is the necessity for clarification of the Code of Guidance in a number of grey areas. This has been partially done in the 1991 revision. For discussion of the changes necessary in the view of interested bodies see the Institute of Housing's report (1989) and many publications by Shelter and CHAR. All organizations have commented that the Code should have statutory force and that there should be an independent appeals system. Some favour appeals through the County Court and others setting up Housing Courts or Tribunals. It is not intended to comment at length on the Code, but attention is drawn to the inconsistencies in Tracey's case.

Tracey's case

The fact that Tracey was not considered to be at risk when she approached the Council after being evicted from her bed-sit shows the uncertainty as to what circumstances constitute special vulnerability. There is also ambiguity about who is responsible for under-18-year-olds, social services or housing departments. Evans and Duncan (1988) found that less than a fifth of authorities in their survey accepted young single applicants on the basis of age alone, despite the content of the Code of Guidance (Para 2.12.ciii 1983 6–13 1991). A check list in the Code for what might be special reasons would help to eliminate some inconsistencies between authorities.

On the second time she presented herself as homeless her experience of sexual harassment and the fact of her pregnancy should have meant acceptance under the Code (Para 2.12.d 1983 6.2 1991). However, some authorities will only accept evidence of a pregnancy after 6 months to ensure that there is certainty of a continuing pregnancy. This is illegal. The code states that a pregnant woman has priority need irrespective of the length of the pregnancy. However, there seems to be some concern that if the pregnancy is terminated, for whatever reason, the woman could still be entitled to be re-housed. Guidance is needed on the timing of serving the required notice (Housing Act, 1985, s.64) informing a pregnant woman of her acceptance as a homeless person. Loss of entitlement to a home seems a harsh penalty on top of loosing a baby.

The matter of the sexual harassment is within the grey area of vulnerability. This also requires a check list in the Code of those people who may be vulnerable. There might also have been racial harassment, which is sometimes difficult to prove, but the word of the harassed person should always be accepted (Chapter 2). Her final attempt at acceptance was successful through the womens' refuge, a refuge worker would have accompanied her to the relevant office. The presence of a refuge worker strengthens an application, for only 30% of authorities accepted a woman as a homeless person on the word of the woman alone, 47% find other evidence 'useful', and 17% definitely wish for other evidence (Evans and Duncan, 1988). At each attempt by Tracey to become accepted as a homeless person it can be seen that because the Act and the Code of Guidance are not specific enough authorities could interpret the rules narrowly. Added to this she had little knowledge of the procedures relating to homelessness, a matter which can only be put right by teaching in the schools on housing rights and increasing publicity of the housing service itself.

5.6 Housing options

5.6.1 Limitations

The housing alternatives open to Tracey at different points in her housing history were constrained by either her income level or the rules governing access to housing in local authorities or housing associations. As a young person entering employment her income would have been low, and being a woman her earnings would be considerably lower than her male counterpart. Annual figures in the New Earnings Survey shows that such disparities continue. Added to this the fact that she was black meant that her chance of finding employment was less than the white majority, and is now compounded by a penal income support system for young people. Some general comments on the latter point and the housing benefit system will be useful before discussing the housing alternatives more fully.

The Social Security Act (1986) instituted major changes in the system of benefits. The present system is supposedly simplified and more accurately targeted on those in need. The 1986 Act introduced:

• a new housing benefit scheme;
• an income support scheme to replace supplementary benefit;
• the social fund instead of single payments;
• family credit instead of family income supplement;
• various other detailed changes to social security benefits.

The three main means-tested benefits (income support, family credit and housing benefit) are now commonly assessed on gross income although there are some differences of detail in the amounts which can be disregarded for the different benefits. It is not intended to discuss in detail the workings of the system. Publications by CHAR, Shelter and the Institute of Housing are useful to keep up to date. However, the key elements in relation to Tracey's situation are the levels of benefit at different ages, the entitlement to board and lodgings allowances, and the use of the social fund. Prior to the Act she would have been entitled to supplementary benefit, housing benefit, board and lodging allowances and single payments. These amounts would have enabled her to pay for bed-and-breakfast, the hostel and womens' refuge and to have claimed housing benefit whilst she was in private rented and short-life housing. Albeit this could not have led to riotous living but would have covered the necessities. The single payments would have enabled her to buy the basic items for her permanent housing with the Council. Now the situation would be completely different. As a single claimant under 25 years old her income support would be only £25.55 as against £41.85. This is not a reasonable amount to pay for all necessities apart from housing. In areas of high rent, where perhaps the housing benefit ceiling is below the maximum rent levels, this tiny living allowance would be further eroded. It is also eroded by the rule change making claimants pay 20% of their Community Charge (Poll Tax). These same arguments apply when low paid employment is obtained. The payment of Board and Lodging allowances to those people staying in hostels or bed-and-breakfast hotels have been reduced along with the general level of benefits. The White Paper, *Caring for People* (Cmnd. 849, 1989) proposes radical changes to the organization and funding of community care, which also affect many hostel users.

The uncertainty and smallness of income sources obviously affects the alternatives available. Tracey had a limited choice of housing in the private sector when she left her friends house. This was a cheap flat in a HMO, or a bed-and-breakfast hotel or a hostel. These and other alternatives that she used later on will be discussed in turn as folllows:

- houses in Multiple Occupation (HMOs) and Private Renting (PR);
- short Stay hostels;
- short life housing;
- womens' refuges;
- permanent housing with local authorities.

5.6.2 HMOs and PR

Tracey's occupation of these options had to be supported by state benefits of some kind. The level of such benefits does not leave surplus to improve the physical surroundings. In most cases the type of housing is undesirable because of overcrowding, cramped rooms, dampness, sharing the facilities or harassment by the landlord or other occupants. Surprisingly, overcrowding is not a problem outside the bed-and-breakfast sector of HMOs, according to an Association of Metropolitan Authorities survey (1987a). In effect 67% of tenants have bed-sits with space standards above Part 10 of the Housing Act 1985. The Housing Act (1969 s.58) states that 'a house which is occupied by persons who do not form a single household' is a house in multiple occupation. The Courts have further defined a wide variety of housing as HMOs. They include housing used on a shared basis, hostels and hotels (Campaign for Bed-Sit Rights, 1989).

Despite overcrowding being an historical concern of local authorities, intervention is minimal and usually follows a complaint about the state of the property. Some local authorities are attempting to inspect and upgrade the

HMOs in their district using the grant system and the powers of management and control given to them by the Housing Act (1985). This enables an authority to serve different types of orders which result in regulating the numbers of occupants, replacing amenities, insisting on defects being repaired and, in the final instance, taking over control of the property. Sadly vigorous action is not always practicable. The loss of living space in these properties can lead to an increase in homelessness or a game of musical chairs for tenants when the landlord is pressed to improve standards.

It is when life becomes unbearable for the tenants that the housing department becomes involved, either through homelessness or the necessity for advice on benefits or the law. Tracey's case is typical of many young people who refer themselves to bed-and-breakfast hotels and the true number is not known (Thomas and Ninier, 1989). Many people who have self-referred themselves to hotels or are living in poor private rented or multi-occupied property will have placed themselves on a Council or Housing Association waiting list. Housing visitors when checking applications have an opportunity to report on conditions and ensure that action is initiated by the Environmental Health Officer. The AMA report *Multiple Occupation a Time for Action* (1987) suggests that the scale of the problem is such that urgent action is needed, that a comprehensive, corporate and co-ordinated approach be taken by local authorities. There is a case for the transfer of all responsibilities to the housing department and at least for far more liaison between the Environmental Health and Housing staff. A further recommendation by the AMA report builds on this idea and suggests that a separate committee be established to pursue this work and be answerable to the Housing Committee.

If given such a reponsibility, housing departments would have to plan a survey of properties and review their re-housing policies. As an interim measure 'A team of tenancy relations officers should be employed to respond to tenants complaints of harassment or illegal eviction' (AMA, 1987) and to help when displacement happens. Counterbalancing this activity landlords should be informed of their reponsibilities to tenants and to properties.

In the private rented sector the levels of rent continue to be a bar to many prospective tenants. Rent levels have been pushed upwards by the deregulation of rents and the introduction of Assured and Assured Shorthold Tenancies*. The rise in house prices has led to the temptation for landlords to sell for capital gain, and has led on occasion to harassment to gain vacant possession. The law has been tightened in this respect by the Housing Act 1988 s.29 although the Association of Tenancy Relations Officers is sceptical of an increase in the conviction rate (Stearn, 1988). The local authorities do

---

* 'Assured' and 'Assured shorthold' tenancies were introduced in the Housing Act (1988). They are a form of tenancy under which market rents can be charged and security of tenure was reduced.

Table 5.4 Type of hostel, by type of organization

| Type of organization | | Voluntary sector | | Public sector | | |
| | All vol. | Independent | Parent/ partner | All public | Local authority | Stat. bail |
% of hostels	84	35	50	16	9	6
Housing only	18	14	20	35	63	–
General	10	8	11	2	3	–
Women's refuges	20	42	5	8	14	–
Offenders	20	16	23	37	–	100
Infirm/Drug/alcohol	14	10	18	14	31	–
All	17	9	22	6	10	–
(Sample size)	(261)	(114)	(147)	(59)	(42)	(14)

Health authority hostels are not shown separately.
Source: Bethoud and Casey (1988) *The Cost of Care in Hostels.* PSI.

help with advice through Housing Aid Centres, debt counselling sections such as the one in Northampton (Embury and Silver, 1989) and financial support to independent money advice centres as in Birmingham. Apart from advice-giving the Housing Act 1988 s.130 has given local authorities wider duties to serve and enforce repair notices under Part V1 of the Housing Act 1985 where properties are unfit, and stronger powers when they are in serious disrepair.

5.6.3 Short stay hostels

Technically, short stay hostels can be classified as HMOs but must have specific social objectives which are distinct from bed-and-breakfast hotels and bed-sit lettings. Entry to a short stay hostel might have been an alternative for Tracey and her baby when she left work at the hotel. Specific hostels have been set up by organizations to meet the need of young unmarried mothers. Advice and support is also given until such time as they can move on to permanent housing. Most hostels of this nature are run by local authorities in conjunction with the social services or church groups. A variety of bodies run other types of hostels. A useful study of hostels has been written by Berthoud and Casey (1988) giving an insight into the diversity of financing and organization. Table 5.4 gives some indication of the variation in type and organization of hostels from Berthoud and Casey's survey of 320 projects. The majority are run by voluntary organizations according to the survey, although 16% are in the public sector and run by local housing departments and local probation committees. The survey commented 'Nearly a quarter of hostels and 50% of hostel residents were found in Greater

London. A relatively large proportion of hostels in London concentrate on provision of housing only. In Scotland there were few hostels for ex-offenders and many for the infirm'.

Hostels differ in their objectives, some provide short or medium term housing for those people unable to live on their own in ordinary housing and often needing an element of care. Others exist to meet the housing needs of people who have experienced social and economic problems and who require advice and assistance for a period of time, for example, homeless persons. Most have been set up specifically to provide care and housing for groups of vulnerable people such as young mothers and babies, ex-offenders, young single people, women who have experienced violence, people with mental health problems or alcohol or drug addictions and people with learning difficulties.

Access to and management of hostels

Tracey gained access to her hostel by self-referral but she could have done so via a referring agency such as the Homeless Persons Unit, probation officers, hospital or social services departments. She was interviewed at the hostel and a decision taken to admit her. Her case was straightforward but it is a fine judgement in the case of residents likely to exhibit disruptive behaviour in a hostel which is regarded by other people as their home. When referrals are made, failure to pass on information about violent individuals can result in disaster. It is, therefore, essential to have clear admission criteria and relevant personal information to enable staff to make consistent judgements. Equal opportunities for women, black people, disabled people and gay men and lesbians must be considered in this area as in all others. Positive action can be taken in the form of encouragement for self-referral by placing advertisements where under-represented groups meet, by employing black staff, using specific referral agencies and setting and monitoring admission targets. Housing management staff should be aware of the access criteria of the hostels in their area, the needs of the occupants for move-on housing and the difficulties which might be encountered when hostel users are eventually housed in permanent homes.

Housing management staff are usually involved in the maintenance of the hostel property, rather than in the day-to-day management of the people. If responsibilty for the whole project lies within a housing organization, specialist staff are employed to run the hostel. More often there is a partnership with a voluntary organization. An independent working party report (NFHA, 1985) and Cope (1990) describes and criticizes such partnerhips.

5.6.4 Short-life housing

Short-life housing is a decreasing option for people like Tracey and her friend when they wanted to live together. Families tend to be given preference over young single people. They had approached a housing association who managed short-life housing and been offered a house repaired to a minimum standard. It was let to them unfurnished, on a low rent and with a licence to occupy. The expectation was that they would move out when the date for rehabilitation was decided. An alternative would have been to link up with a group who liaised with such an association.

In the 1980s, central government cut capital monies for rehabilitation and building programmes leaving local authorities unable to complete their programmes and housing associations with a build-up of homes in their development pipeline. There has been considerable criticism of local authorities by central government because Council properties have remained empty, despite the main reason being deliberate starvation of funds from the centre. In any case the major culprits have been private owners and the central government's own departments, for example, the Ministry of Defence (NAO, 1987). This does not mean that local authorities were not at fault in some respects. In the 1970s, when homelessness was beginning to increase sharply, local authorities were reluctant to use vacant properties needing major repairs for short-life housing and gave homeless squatters short shrift. Now there is more likely to be co-operation between squatting groups and councils, or making use of housing associations to manage short-life housing for occupation by homeless people. Monies given to the local authorities and to housing associations in the form of MINI-HAG have been used to improve short-life properties to a higher standard of temporary repair. It is a sensible option but unfortunately, it does not help to increase the supply of homes significantly, which is at the heart of the problem.

Management of short-life housing

Short-life housing can be managed in four ways:

Within the Housing Department

In Niner's study (1989) she found that 'Islington had about 260 units in the Council stock awaiting improvement or Estate Action or on acquired property awaiting rehabilitation'. Similarly, Hillingdon and New Forest used purpose-built council housing awaiting major repairs. All three councils managed the property directly and let to occupiers on an unprotected licence.

By registered housing associations on behalf of local authorities

Niner's study showed that Cardiff council had three houses handed over to an association for managing, whilst the Emergency Property Organization in

London managed large numbers of properties on behalf of a variety of London Boroughs. Management contracts set out the likely length of time for which licences may be granted and cash limits on the repair work allowed. Nominations are made to the associations from the relevant department for either bed-and-breakfast users or homeless persons. Housing associations in London charge a management fee of £50 per week per property, which is still cheaper than bed-and-breakfast hotels.

Local authorities letting to a short-life group

This can be done in a similar way to letting to a housing association. The group receives the licence and makes out another direct licence with the occupier.

By housing associations using their own development programme houses

When associations use properties in their own development programmes, management is more complicated. The ability to carry out work at a time convenient to the association is crucial to the development programme. A study of housing associations in London (Williams and Mountford-Smith, 1989) found that many associations have a relaxed attitude towards squatters, making arrangements to evict them only as the properties were needed.

Sometimes there is antipathy from the housing management staff of an association towards using development 'voids'* for this purpose. Management questions of levels of repair, collection of rents and finally eviction proceedings take up a disproportionate amount of time in relation to other association tenants and properties. Affording the repairs to properties is also a problem which is affected by government funding strategies and factors such as inflation and interest rates. There are severe disadvantages to families if left in occupation for a long time, particularly the women and young children who spend long periods in the home. Despite these problems the balance of interest appears to be for such properties to be put to short-life use, with the caveat that it should clearly be a stepping stone to permanent housing.

5.6.5 Womens' refuges

After her stay in the mother and baby home, Tracey met a male partner and went to live with him in his local authority flat. The economic difficulties

---

* 'Void' is a general term used for empty houses or flats waiting to be renovated or relet. A 'development void' is a property in the ownership of a housing association waiting to be renovated.

raised by having a second child produced tensions which resulted in both her child by her first partner and herself being battered. The avenues of escape from such a situation are via relatives, friends or womens' refuges or local authorities. Relatives and friends can only help for a limited period of time and of course this temporary haven is known to the violent partner. Some councils have a policy of automatically re-housing in permanent housing women who experience violence but such a response cannot always be quick or easy. The aim of Womens' Aid is firstly to provide an emergency safe place for women and their children who have suffered physical or mental violence and give them support when they have decided to leave permamently, and secondly, give advice and support to any woman who asks for it. The role of the womens' refuge is quite widely known but access to one is, again, dependent on where a person lives. Welsh Womens' Aid (1986) produced a report which stated that there were 26 affiliated refuges, two independent ones and some groups offering advice. This number was well short of the need based on the recommendation of the 1975 Select Committee on Violence in Marriage of 1 family place per 10 000 population.

Refuges are always managed by a voluntary group but the provision of the buildings may be by either a housing association or a local authority, similarly to hostel provision. Properties tend to be older and large which means maintenance can become a problem. Designing the interior to cater for the needs of a number of families calls for ingenuity. The addresses are kept secret, for obvious reasons, and one member of the housing staff of the landlord will be a designated contact manager, preferably a woman. She will be reponsible for all liaison between the association and the refuge and will order repairs, deal with complaints, collect rent, etc. The telephone number of the refuge must be known to agencies who will be approached by women needing help, but every effort is made to stop the address becoming generally known. Housing staff should be trained in the approach to be taken in advising abused women so that inappropriate legal remedies such as injunctions (Eardley, 1989) are not suggested. The major problem for the users of the refuges as for all short stay hostels is access to permanent housing and it is this 'move-on' aspect together with resettlement practices that will be discussed in the next section.

5.6.6 Permanent housing and resettlement

A problem common for all short stay hostels and short-life residents is that of gaining access to permanent housing. The time which Tracey was forced to spend in the hostel and the refuge was partially due to the lack of 'move-on' housing. The moving on of residents must take place or the system clogs up. Some groups, such as the young single person or people with mental health problems, will also need help in resettling in a permanent home.

Eardley's report (1989) details a clear picture of who inhabits hostels in London and their needs in terms of move-on housing. A wider view is obtained from Niner's study of homelessness (1989). These two studies will serve to give the general picture. In London there is a desperate shortage of move-on housing, Eardley's survey found that 'Existing hostels and projects need an estimated minimum of 7030 units of permanent move-on housing for their residents in 1988/89 and at least a further 8000 in 1989/90. 80% of units required are needed in inner London'. Various strategies are adopted to en-courage the free flow of residents. A quota system is operated by a number of housing associations and local authorities to house a fixed number of re-sidents directly from the hostels in a given year. It is possible that these quotas are not always met but at least the right to a nomination is established. Eardley's report found that approximately 50% of the London Boroughs operated a quota system but only 50% of these fulfilled their quota. Shame-fully, gender and ethnic minority monitoring was not carried out on any scale, but the findings of Eardley's survey suggest an imbalance in the housing of black and ethnic minority residents. This is pertinent to someone like Tracey.

Other solutions involve consortia of or individual housing associations who will accept nominations from the local authorities. In Derbyshire there is an example of a consortium of local authorities who pool a specific number of houses for the use of homeless persons and those coming from hostels. On occasion a short-life housing organization which is a fully mutual co-op can expand into privately financed permanent housing. This may be done with the help of a housing association or secondary co-op.

In London there was also access to housing via nominations from mobility schemes outside the general lettings of associations and authorities. These schemes were the London Area Mobility Scheme (LAMS), the Greater London Mobility Scheme (GLMS) the Inner Borough Nominations Scheme (IBNS) and the Housing Association Liaison Office (HALO), all of which have now been merged into 'Homes'. In other parts of the country consortia of housing assocations and boroughs have been set up. For example, in Nottingham and Sheffield city-wide hostels and homeless forums meet with representatives from hostels, associations, authorities, etc. to discuss problems and imple-ment solutions.

Support workers

A growing feature is the availability of support workers in moving from hostels, which would have been of value to Tracey. An interesting project has been started under the auspices of the Leeds Shaftesbury Project (LSP). Local housing associations have given 2% of their properties to the LSP to manage, which will be used to rehouse hostel residents. LSP will offer support to residents through a housing support worker until they are ready to become direct tenants of the associations, at which stage the property will be handed back and replaced by another. The idea of initial support for residents on taking up a tenancy has been followed by a number of authorities. Sheffield has a tenancy support worker scheme for single homeless, but finds that the workloads for the staff are very high, thus defeating the object of the exercise. The Glasgow Homemaker scheme is run along the same lines.

Niner's survey of authorities identified a number of problems with which prospective tenants will need help at the resettlement period. The Social Fund rules are causing particular problems to those people leaving hostels. Very few will have the capital to buy furniture, bedding, etc., and will, therefore, be dependent on a loan or grant from the Fund. Homelessness officers often help their clients to fill up the forms, chase DSS and explore other avenues for furniture. Various schemes were set up specifically to help clients. Niner reports that 'Newcastle had set up a Single Persons Support Team, a unit of three staff, with a specific brief of helping young single people to take up and retain a tenancy'. Similarly 'Birmingham had Family Support Workers who helped hostel residents with the assembly of furniture or other things connected with the move'. Islington went a step further in authorizing officers to buy cookers and beds to allow people to move in without waiting for DHSS grants. These services will continue, and in some cases authorities and associations will return to the practice of retaining a furniture store (HA Weekly, 1.12.89). The help of support workers in obtaining grants and loans from the Social Fund will be vital. In the future Community Care Grants may help to overcome some of the problems.

Apart from the administrative headaches of settling people into their new homes, individuals will need support in learning how to manage a home in terms of budgeting, dealing with payment of bills and household tasks. Many young people will never have had experience in these matters. Other people suffering with mental health problems may need emotional support for a period of time until used to the new environment. This supportiveness is a costly process but will mean more contented tenants and, balanced against social and economic costs in the long term, is well worthwhile.

Conclusions

Tracey's housing history is not unusual. The lack of supply of new housing means that more and more people are being pushed into experiencing homelessness. The health of this group of people is in jeopardy, particularly the children. Local authorities are being driven by the lack of resources to tighten the rules relating to priority for acceptance as homeless. If a person's income is low, access to housing is severely restricted and if not accepted as homeless the alternative is sleeping rough or depending on friends and relatives. This is leading to an overcrowding problem and increasing strain on family relations. Bed-and-breakfast hotels, hostels and short-life properties are on the whole emergency or short stay provision, and there is a desperate need for move-on housing. However, there can only be a limited response by housing organizations.

Central government has pinned its hopes on the private sector producing the necessary supply of housing for owner occupation, and has reduced monies for public housing provision. The theory is that some council tenants will move out to make way for the low income groups and that housing associations will be the prime providers of new social housing. Everyone else will be expected to afford their own homes. In November 1989 extra money was brought forward from the 1990/91 allocation but was inadequate and soon spent and further sums have been given in 1991. The introduction of the Local Government and Housing Act 1989 has further complicated the financing of local government and reduced the flexibility of authorities to meet their duty to rehouse the homeless. Housing Associations cannot meet the need quickly, and sustained growth will eventually lead them to becoming similar to local authorities. The options open to Tracey at various times in her housing progress look like being the only options for people like her for some time to come.

6

Participation and power in housing

6.1 Introduction

This chapter discusses the means of entry to the housing ladder and how individuals may participate in and gain some control of their housing situation. The various possible ways of gaining control are first listed, split into individualistic and collective approaches, and the case history of the Morley family is then outlined. The discussion commences with a review of the definitions of participation. The law on participation is then looked at, noting the statutory requirements for information availability, tenant consultation and tenant representation. The second part of the discussion focuses on the non-statutory problems that applicants like the Morleys face, with reference to the importance of adequate information, waiting list rules, waiting list unwritten rules and, for Housing Associations, the possible problems in the additional avenues of nominations, referrals and advertising. The list is rounded out by discussion of the remaining options of ownership, co-operatives of all the various types and self-building schemes. The third part looks at the avenues for participation, first noting the considerable advantages for all in good tenant involvement. Pre-allocation participation is discussed, and the values and possible problems of an active Tenants' Association reviewed. Representation on committees, of both Local Authorities and Housing Associations, is then looked at, and finally the idea of tenant management coops is discussed.

The Morley's housing history highlights the lack of individual power of people to gain access to the housing system. Successful entry is wholly dependent on either housing circumstances matching criteria erected by a housing organization, or by having sufficient money to purchase a home. Once entry is gained to the system there is some chance of influencing or ulitmately

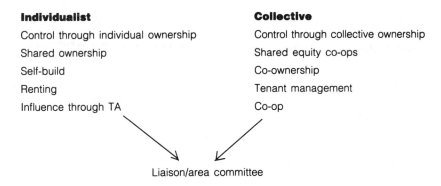

Figure 6.1 Housing solutions.

controlling one's housing. The housing solutions achieved may be through either individual or collective means. Figure 6.1 shows their possible choices.

The highest level of control is retained by the individual owner. Collective owners may experience tensions when the individuals suppress self-interest. Least control is experienced by the renter whether individually or collectively. The ways and means of how an individual may participate in the control of their housing is the subject of this chapter.

PROFILE C

Tim and Ann Morley live in a large northern city. They married in 1985 and registered their names on the housing waiting list of the local council. Ann became pregnant but they had to continue living at their respective parent's homes as the council could not offer them anywhere to live. Their many attempts to find private rented housing were unsuccessful and their income of £144 per week was not high enough to enable them to buy a home. Relationships inevitably became very strained between the partners, and between them and their parents. A second pregnancy made the situation desperate. Through friends they heard of a one bedroom flat above a shop, which was in a row due for redevelopment. It was in very poor condition, and no place to bring up children. However, they decided to apply for it and were lucky enough to get it. The let was for a period of one year and in that time they had hoped they would receive an offer of a house from the Council. By this time their names had been on the waiting list for about eighteen months with a prospective wait of another two and a half years. In the same area as the flat a community-based housing association functioned which publicized its presence via neighbourhood groups, leaflets, etc. The Morleys heard of the Association and approached them for help. They were told that their only chance of being housed was for the council to nominate them to the Association, as their own list was closed. They returned to the council's Housing Department and enquired about the possibility of a nomination. They were told that they were quite high on the list, but that there were many people in a similar position. They were also told that decants* from a big modernization scheme took precedence over homeless families, who were only being offered bed-and-breakfast places.

In some despair, as the poor condition of the flat was aggravating the asthmatic condition of their older child, they reluctantly asked their parents if they could return to live with them. At intervals they badgered the council for help. Having to live separately had raised their total of 'housing points' and they felt that the stress levels experienced by them all should add extra points. They contacted the Association again, and were told that although the list was closed nominees would be accepted from the council for a housing scheme of 24 houses and 12 flats which was being built. They decided to approach their local councillor for help to be considered as a 'special case', and ask their doctor to submit medical evidence to the housing department. As a result of these moves, their application was considered at the 'special case' committee. Their application was successful and their name was nominated to the Association.

The Association was implementing a policy of allocating homes at an early stage in the building process, so that prospective tenants might contribute to design. The Morleys, therefore, had an opportunity to influence the siting of kitchen equipment, type of heating, colours of the interior and exterior painting, etc. Their excitement was considerable and made the remaining months living apart bearable. In due course, they moved into one of the houses and lived there happily for three years.

As a result of participation in the design consultation exercise, Ann became interested in joining the management committee of the association. Through the staff she found out that any tenant involvement was welcome and she was duly nominated and elected to the committee. As there was no tenants' association she could not act in a representatvie capacity, but her contribution as a tenant was invaluable. She had the opportunity to attend training courses and conferences and began to become interested in the idea of 'tenant co-operatives'. She canvassed her neighbours in the houses and flats and found a few like-minded spirits who were open to the suggestion of considering a management co-op. They approached the association who were supportive of the idea. It was more difficult to convince other neighbours of the attractions of a co-op as some had long terms plans to buy their properties and others saw no point in taking over the responsibilities of the Housing Association.

---

* Decant is the jargon word for a tenant who has to be moved either temporarily or permanently from their home to another property whilst repairs or modernization takes place.

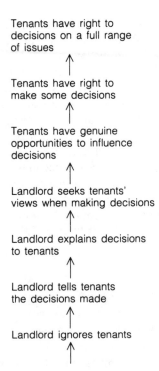

Tenants have right to
decisions on a full range
of issues

Tenants have right to
make some decisions

Tenants have genuine
opportunities to influence
decisions

Landlord seeks tenants'
views when making decisions

Landlord explains decisions
to tenants

Landlord tells tenants
the decisions made

Landlord ignores tenants

Figure 6.2   Tenant involvement ladder.
Source: Guidelines for Tenant Involvement. Labour Housing Group (1989).

The discussion led, however, to the setting up of a Tenants' Association which actively influenced the policies of the Association. This was followed by the establishment of a management co-op. The Morleys became active members of the co-op and like many others found it a satisfying way of controlling their own housing.

Before discussing the alternatives open to the Morleys and how they achieved some measure of control over their own housing, it is necessary to define participation and look at the law in relation to it.

6.2   Definition of participation

Participation is a broad concept and people interpret its meaning very differently. A very simple definition might be the ways in which a citizen is able to take part in the formulation and implementation of policies. Figure 6.2 shows a useful ladder of 'tenant involvement' which reflects various levels at which this might take place. It moves from the point where the landlord totally ignores the tenant upto the point where tenants have a right to make decisions on a whole range of issues.

It is hoped that all landlords will seek to involve their tenants in some way, but different rungs will be appropriate at different times and tenants may wish to participate at different levels.

A more detailed definition has been advanced by the IOH/TPAS (1989). They suggest that it is 'A two way process involving sharing of information and ideas, where tenants are able to influence decisions and take part in what is happening'. The Community Development Housing Group (1986), promoted a broader definition which was 'the involvement of tenants in decisions which affect their housing'. This definition has been expanded by Platt *et al.* (1987) to 'the right of tenants to have a say in decisions which affect their housing and the opportunity to review the consequences that flow from them'. The emphasis in each definition is subtly different, tilting to either landlord or tenant, depending on which organization is promulgating it. Whichever definition is used, it is important that it is agreed by all the parties involved in any participatory exercise.

6.3 The law and tenants' participation

In the last ten years the law relating to tenant participation in housing has been strengthened, but commitment to its implementation is varied. A legal right to consultation on housing management matters was first introduced by The Housing Act (1980). This 'tenants' charter' formalized a number of activities already being carried out by the more enlightened authorities and associations. The following list of Acts are the principal statutes defining the duties and rights of landlords and tenants in relation to tenant participation.

- Housing Act (1985) (consolidates the Housing Act 1980);
- Housing (Scotland) Act (1987);
- Housing and Planning Act (1986);
- Housing Act (1988);
- Housing (Scotland) Act (1988).

Information

Effective participation requires information. The law regarding the provision of information for purposes of consultation is sparse. However, s.105 of the Housing Act 1988 requires that secure tenants be both informed and consulted about proposed changes in any housing management matters which will affect them substantially. Housing management is defined as matters which relate to every day management, maintenance, improvement, demolition and the provision of services or amenities. It should be noted that the crucial matters of rent and service charges are excluded from the definition. The tenants' views must be considered, but the catch is that the arrangements for doing this are left entirely to the discretion of the housing organization, though where adopted they must be published.

Housing associations must additionally send copies of these consultation arrangements to the Housing Corporation and the relevant Local Authority. Copies of all these arrangements must be available for inspection at no charge or a reasonable charge for purchase.

Similarly the rules and procedures for the allocation of housing by any organization must be published and/or made available for inspection (Housing Act 1988 s.106). New Town Development Corporations also have to conform to these requirements.

Assured tenants of housing associations have similar rights under the Housing Act (1988) as required by the Tenants' Guarantee published by the Housing Corporation (43/1988). The guarantee has similar rules to the statutory rights of secure tenants.

Scotland has slightly different arrangements, under the Housing (Scotland) Act (1987). For secure tenants the law requires authorities and associations to draw up a written lease, (s.53) and both parties have the right to approach the Sheriff's Court over failures to agree changes. Assured tenants of housing associations in Scotland have to depend on the goodwill of associations following the model tenancy agreement produced by the Scottish Federation of Housing Associations.

The 1986 Housing Act removed the control tenants had on holding on to their home. Prior to this tenants could only be moved against their will if repairs and maintenance on their home were to be carried out. After the Act Councils could empty estates and sell them off with a consultation exercise as the only right of the tenants to influence the matter (s.6). Research conducted by Glendinning, Allen and Young (1989) on authority house sales to the private sector, confirmed this. A large majority (82%) of the 'decanted' tenants said that they had not been asked for their opinion and when it had been sought it was only commonly by a public meeting.

The Housing Act (1988)

The final piece of legislation, the Housing Act 1988, does not directly enhance the rights of tenants to consultation. The government's stated intention behind the legislation was to offer local authority tenants a choice of landlord, (White Paper, CM 214), but it is seen by many as a method of dismantling municipal housing. It was thought that the greatest danger to this might come from HATs. But the Secretary of State can only agree to a transfer after a consultation by a ballot and if a majority of all the tenants entitled to vote agree.

Consultation by ballot is also required for transfer under 'Tenants' choice'.*

---

* Tenants' choice. The phrase used to cover the provisions in the Housing Act (1988) allowing tenants to chose an alternative landlord.

However, the rules are different for counting votes for these (s.102 and s.103). An application for transfer can proceed if half the tenants entitled to vote have done so and one half of these agreed to the transfer. Thus 25% of the total tenants can swing a decision because with such a system all non-voters are counted as 'Yes' votes. These rules also apply if tenants form an organization to become a landlord. The Housing (Scotland) Act (1988) is broadly the same but s.58 allows individual tenants to agree to or prevent their house being acquired by a prospective new landlord.

Some authorities are bypassing the whole system by transferring empty properties to new landlords, 'trickle transfer' being the phrase coined.

Decision making

In addition to the above duties, authorities and associations have discretion to involve tenants in the formal decision-making committees of their organizations. Authorities are bound by Acts of Parliament, namely, the Local Government Act (1972), the Local Government (Scotland) Act (1973) and the Local Government and Housing Act (1989). The latter act prevents co-opted members of housing committees or sub-committees from voting. However, tenants are permitted to vote on Advisory committees. So much for tenant power. Although housing associations are encouraged to empower tenants, they can only go as far as their rules permit. A survey of associations in December 1987 by the Community Rights Project found that 'Many associations have rules which impede openess and tenant participation. Some do not even fulfil their statutory responsibilities. Some associations, however, have spent time and money promoting tenant involvement' (CRP and CAG, 1987). This state of affairs will not be able to continue. The Housing Corporation intends to monitor the progress of 'tenant participation' as part of the regular assessment of the effectiveness of associations (HC, 1989).

Other sections in the Act (s.10 and s.11) enable tenants' associations, in certain circumstances, to force authorities to consider the establishment of a management or ownership co-op and enter into a management agreement.

Fuller details of the legal requirements for authorities and associations in relation to tenant particapation can be found in the IOH/TPAS publication (1989).

6.4 Housing access — the information difficulties for an applicant

Rules govern the entry to all housing except that of individual owner occupation, which is governed by price. The first problem of the Morleys was how to gain accesss to any tenure. They had no money to purchase a house so they had to look to renting. Their initial housing circumstances did not meet the criteria of need set by the Council to grant immediate re-housing, so they could only put themselves on the waiting list.

It is important to note that at this point of trying to enter the housing ladder the Morleys, in common with most such applicants, had no real chance of exerting influence to make the rules more flexible or fair. Any pressures for change in the entry criteria tends to come from external, organized bodies like research groups and the professional bodies in the housing field.

In trying to assess their position the Morleys first faced the problem of finding sufficient information to make a sensible judgement about their options, particularly their chances of Council accommodation. For the rules governing the Council waiting list — and this can equally apply to housing associations' waiting lists — the Morleys were dependent on the receptionist in the housing office, published pieces of paper or word of mouth. They did receive an information pack which included many details of the eligibility rules, but notably it did not include mention of any appeal procedure against refusal of entry to the system.

Technically it could be argued that the Morleys used the 'special case' system as a method of appeal when they belatedly found out that their child's asthma entitled them to special consideration. But its specific absence from the published rules is a cause for concern.

Research has shown that not all authorities publish summaries of their allocations policies or attempt to inform the public at large (Glasgow University, 1989). It would have been useful to the Morleys to have had a greater spread of information sources. Their Council might have:

- fulfilled its legal obligations by publishing a summary of the rules for allocations;
- made sure that the summary was available in public libraries, community centres, citizens advice bureau, housing aid centres, benefits shops, etc.;
- actively contacted neighbourhood groups, black and Asian groups, hostels, and voluntary organizations to publicise the Authority's housing policies and to assess the local need;
- contacted schools and talked to 15 and 16 year olds about the realities of finding housing if they leave home;
- used the local media, i.e. radio, newspapers and community broadsheets, as publicity avenues.

Beyond this the mere fact that basic information is available does not mean that the allocations system is properly understood. People find it difficult to understand why they cannot have complete choice of district or type of property, or why they have to wait so long.

6.4.1 Hidden rules

In addition to the published rules some Councils also have an informal rule that applicants must be on the waiting list for a set period of time before being considered for a home. There can be other reasons influencing the way an allocations policy is operated. The housing chances of the Morleys will have been affected by some of the following factors:

- conflicts between central and local government;
- professional ideology;
- tenant resources;
- patterns of choice open to tenants;
- characteristics of the stock in a situation of limited supply;
- relative bargaining power of different groups to obtain housing in different types of stock. An example is the precedence that decanted tenants have over homeless people;
- eligibility rules, points schemes;
- grading of applicants;
- dispersal policies in relation to black applicants;
- direct and indirect discrimination.

Malpass and Murie usefully summarize the relevant research. They comment the 'The research literature has increasingly complemented reference to administrative and professional discretion such as "grading" with references to shortages and supply factors which heavily constrain allocation' (Malpass and Murie, 1987).

Chapter 3 discussed some of these factors more fully. Two recent studies Glasgow University (1989) and Prescott-Clarke *et al.* (1988) give useful information describing access policies and procedures in authorities and associations. They should be read in conjunction with the research on homelessness by Thomas and Niner (1989) and Evans and Duncan (1988).

Housing associations too have waiting lists, and the information on them is sometimes even more difficult to find, if it exists at all. The Glasgow University research found that 'housing associations of all sizes were much less likely to have formal schemes which included points or date order priority'. Just over 50% of housing associations assessed applicants individually, points schemes were used by about 26% of associations and the reminder used a date order system.

There are considerable dangers in using a system of individual comparisons of applications involving the discretion of staff or committee members. Applicants find it difficult to understand the logic in the choices and may regard it as an unfair way of allocating housing. It is not always possible to be consistent or unbiased. This is one of the few times that an applicant might successfully try to influence the system by using personal contacts to push forward a claim to housing.

Points schemes only partially achieve objective measurement of an applicant's need. It is, however, an explainable system to the public and a starting point for selection. The factors chosen to represent need in a points scheme will be split between measurable factors like number of persons and rooms, and subjective factors like house condition, medical and social needs which are open to interpretation. They can be given different weighting to correspond with the importance assigned to them by a particular housing committee and staff (Appendix D). The public do not have any say in which factors should be used or how they should be weighted. A date order system does not take account of degree of housing need.

6.4.2 Housing access — the waiting list

The Morleys had no difficulty in simply registering on the list, but had a long wait until they were offered a housing association property. The prime reason for their wait was lack of supply of housing. Evidence from the Glasgow University research (1989) shows that the average number of people on local authority waiting and transfer lists in 1988 was 5182, ranging from an average of 1834 in authorities with less than 5000 properties to an average of 17 787 in authorities with more than 30 000 properties. The average number on Housing Association waiting lists was 583 for local associations and 3671 for regional and national ones.

At the time the Morleys approached the community housing association in their area the waiting list was closed. This occurance is not uncommon in smaller associations where there is a small turnover of lettings and a limited development programme.

All waiting list restrictions particularly work against black and Asian people and young single persons. There is also often a direct exclusion of single people and owner occupiers, although exceptional cases will be considered, for example due to hardship or domestic violence. Research on these problems has been carried out by Prescott-Clarke *et al.*, 1988; Spicker, 1983; Henderson and Karn, 1987; Matthews, 1983.

6.4.3 Housing access — via a housing association

The Morleys gained entry to a housing association through nomination by the Council. The various routes for such entry are:

- nomination;
- referrals from a variety of agencies;
- direct advertising as projects become available;
- a waiting list.

The waiting list has been dealt with in the previous section, but nominations, referrals and direct advertising are more usually associated with Housing Associations.

Nominations

The Morleys were nominated to a Housing Association as a result of their request to be considered a 'special case'. It is only recently that Local Authorities have begun to include a section on their application forms relating to associations and nomination rights. This can be a crucial lack of information to those seeking housing. After the Morleys were nominated they were visited in their own home to verify their circumstances, and only then were they were offered a tenancy. The home visit was also an opportunity to tell the Morleys about the association.

In circular 48/89 of the Housing Corporation, it was laid down that 50% of associations' tenancies should be offered to authorities to nominate their own tenants or applicants from the waiting list. Some associations will accept 100% nominations for their tenancies. The NFHA, the Association of London Authorities and the London Boroughs Association combined in that year to produce a guide to nomination procedures entitled 'Partners in Meeting Need'. The NFHA also combined with the AMA and the ADC to publish a joint statement on local authority nomination which provides a workable framework (NFHA/AMA/ADC 1989).

The safeguarding of the integrity of the objectives of an association whilst trying to meet nomination needs, can lead to friction between it and a Council. For instance a date order system in a Local Authority waiting list would mean that applicants from the authority's list might not be in as great a need as those on the association's list. Surprisingly, a third of nominations in England and Wales have been local authority tenants, whom you might have expected to be well housed, rather better than applicants from the private sector (Randolph and Levison, 1988). One explanation might be that associations operate in inner city areas and will help authorities to house people 'decanted' from estates which are to be refurbished or cleared.

Referrals

The referral system would not have been open to the Morleys as it applies only to people living in hostels, residential homes, hospitals, etc. A small percentage of associations accept people referred by both statutory and non-statutory agencies. The NFHA census of new tenancies (Randolph and Levison, 1988, Table G10) shows that 3% were accepted from statutory agencies and 4% from voluntary ones.

Because of the objectives of an association there may be a direct connection with a specific agency. For example, an association set up to house young black people may take referrals from hostels catering for black homeless youngsters. A womens' refuge (similar to the one where Tracey in Chapter 5 lived) may have a quota with a particular association who house only families.

Some of the agencies involved will offer support services to their clients which will continue when they are housed. This is of advantage to housing association staff as it relieves some of the the the burden of housing management.

When accepting referrals associations must ensure three things. Firstly that those in greatest need are being considered. Secondly that the policies and practices of the referral agencies are compatible with those of the association. Thirdly that equal opportunity policies are observed (NFHA, 1987). This implies that there must be regular monitoring of the agency's objectives.

Direct advertising

In the Morley's case it was old direct advertising that had led them to the association, though at a time when the Association's list was closed. The dir-ect advertising of properties has usually been associated with the letting of unpopular estates. The GLC let some of their blocks of flats by this method. A variation has been the 'sons and daughters' schemes, whereby local letting was encouraged and offers made to the children of existing tenants on an estate. However, these schemes were judged to breach equal opportunity ideals. In the case of associations advertising might be used for specific projects, such as a co-operative, or local letting to elderly people. It is a justifiable method in such cases even when lists have been closed for a period of time, or to reach groups who would not normally register their names. The objectives of the association must still be met, and the people housed still in need.

6.5 Owner occupation

The only way open to the Morleys to obtain housing quickly was some form of purchase. Their income of £144 per week would have supported a mortgage of around £20 000. In some cities in the northern part of the country this would have bought them a small terraced or semi-detached property. In the south east it would not be enough for a deposit. Even if they managed to buy a house or flat, maintaining a home on such a low income would have been difficult. Three cheaper alternative methods of ownership were possible, ownership co-operatives, shared ownership or self-build, and these will be examined in turn with the reasons for the Morley's rejection of each option.

6.5.1 Ownership co-operatives

The reasons given for people entering a co-operative form of housing are various. There is the desire to meet housing need, have collective control, do a better job than the landlord and in some cases use it as a means of gaining full owner-occupation (McCafferty and Riley, 1989). Although these are the underlying reasons for joining a co-operative, the study showed that 'participating' in the work of the co-op was seen as the most important issue.

The form that participation can take is variable, from maintenance tasks to committee work. Table 6.1 shows the pattern of participation in the different types of co-ops.

The McCafferty and Riley study stated that 605 co-ops had been established, 63% of which were ownership co-ops and that there was a high level of overall satisfaction. They are unevenly spread throughout the country, with the majority being in London, the North West and Yorkshire and Humberside. There are three types of ownership co-ops:

- common-ownership;
- shared ownership;
- co-ownership.

Common-ownership

In these types of co-ops the property is held in common by individual members who are both tenants and owners. They do not have an individual stake in the equity. The most common name is a 'Par Value' or 'Non-Equity' co-op where tenants collectively own or lease the property (DOE Circular, 8/76). They take up a nominal £1 share which is returned when they leave the co-op. 'Fair Rent' co-ops have a similar structure but are so-called because they have been established by the system of grants and loans to housing associations and have a rent fixed by the rent officer. The 'right to buy' is not available in these forms of co-ops, which means that they may remain in low cost ownership. They are attractive to single persons in particular, who make up a high proportion of the households in them. This type of co-op would have been possible for the Morleys but none were available in their area.

Shared-ownership

This concept has been developed in recent years, in answer to escalating costs of building. It is more usually applied to individual properties. The property is offered part for sale and part for rent. An example is the Glenkerry Housing Co-op in a tower block in the East End of London, set up by the Greater London Secondary Housing Association for the GLC. It was achieved 'with a complicated formula whereby the local authority own the freehold, the co-op a community leasehold and the flat dwellers 50% of the value of their dwellings. They do not have the right to buy the rest of the equity, and so the co-op will continue to supply low-cost home ownership to those just starting on the owner-occupied ladder' (Birchall 1988).

An alternative scheme is described by Birchall. CDS Co-operative Housing have offered owner-tenants the opportunity to buy 50% to 70% of the

Table 6.1 Tenant involvement in running their co-op

			Type of co-op			
	All co-ops	Local authority tenant management	Housing association tenant management	Par value	Co-ownership	Short-life
Percentage ever involved in:[†]						
Repairing/maintaining own home	42	40	33	39	36	77
Distributing information to members	23	21	22	32	6	34
Organizing social activities	21	18	20	30	14	34
Sub-committees	20	19	20	35	6	20
Maintaining communal areas	20	18	16	21	9	43
Tenant selection	18	15	16	35	5	20
None of these	34	40	40	18	44	11
Base*:	(456)	(219)	(45)	(84)	(64)	(44)

* Excluding co-op officers.

[†] Respondents were presented with a list of 25 activities a member of a co-op might be involved in.

Source: McCafferty, P. and Riley, D. (1989) *A Study of Co-operative Housing*. HMSO. With permission of the Controller HMSO.

equity, initially, and then staircase their way to full ownership in 10% tranches. Members are selected according to their ability to pay. When they leave the scheme they must either find a buyer for their share of the property, or buy the whole of the equity on the same day and sell on to a new member. If the latter method is used there is a danger of the co-op vanishing and being replaced by an owner-occupied estate.

These schemes have helped people on low income such as the Morleys, but as rent levels and house prices rise it will become increasingly difficult for owner-tenants to pay. The Morleys foresaw that the level of their income might be a problem in this co-op. Numerically they have not made much impact on housing provision but the 1989 study found that satisfaction is high, and housing need is being met.

Co-ownership co-ops

In co-ownership co-ops tenants collectively own and manage their property, but can sell their share in the property back to the co-op when they leave. The idea was imported from Scandanavia but never developed in the same way in this country. 'Its form and its function was moulded by the British political context and the overwhelming support for owner occupation as the dominant housing tenure' (Clapham and Kintrea 1987). In the late sixties and early seventies a number of these co-ops were developed by builders, architects and estate agents rather than individual residents. Clapham and Kintrea suggest that the main interest of the professional agents was in the 'professional fees that could be extracted'. Residents found that service costs rose steadily and there were moves by a number of co-ops to take over the management themselves. However, the Housing Act 1980 dealt a fatal blow to this form of housing. It gave co-owners the right to buy the remaining share in their homes at the original market value, and many exercised the right. Co-ownership is being revived to some extent by the 'Pathfinder' and 'Sundowner' schemes of Coventry Churches Housing Association, but was obviously not a suitable option for the Morleys.

Individual shared-ownership

The right to shared ownership was given by The Housing and Building Control Act 1984 s.12 (now consolidated in the Housing Act 1985, s.143). The idea of part owning and part renting is to help people on lower incomes to gain a foot on the ownership ladder. Local authorities, New Towns and Housing Associations were empowered to offer shared ownership where they were selling properties, under the right to buy, building for sale, or homesteading. A long lease is bought for a sum representing 50% or 75% of the value of a property, up to a specified limit. Residents may move to full ownership in stages as they can afford it (DOE revised 1987). This scheme was preceded by 'Do-it-yourself-shared-ownership' (DYSO) which enabled prospective applicants, tenants, or first time buyers to choose a property and acquire it on a shared ownership basis through a housing association. The scheme proved too popular, particularly in areas of high house prices, and the money set aside in the Approved Development Programme of the Housing Corporation was soon spent. The emphasis has now moved to offering tenants discounts to purchase a house on the open market. In 1984, tenants of charitable housing associations were offered 'transferable' discounts roughly equivalent to their entitlement under the 'right-to-buy' (NFHA 1984a). This scheme, known as 'Home ownership for tenants of charitable housing associations' (HOTCHA), was operated by nominated associations and worked within a cash limit on a first come, first served basis. It has also proved popular but the numbers involved are still small. The Morleys might have taken advantage of this scheme as it would have made ownership possible in their part of the country where house prices and rents were lower. The fact that Tim Morley was the sole wage earner made them wary of such a financial commitment at a time when unemployment was high. The Housing Corporation's 1988/89 report states that there were about 600 applicants for HOTCHA discounts. The same report mentions the introduction of a 'Tenants' Incentive Scheme' which will offer a grant to tenants who require limited assistance to purchase in the private market. The latter scheme was given a boost by the government in March 1990 with £36m going directly to associations and permission to borrow £38m was given to authorities for the same purpose (HA Weekly, 30.3.90).

Self Build

Self Build is a way to obtain a new home, at a reasonable cost, but is offset by the time commitment needed to finish a scheme (NFHA 1988). Once again the Morleys felt that the financial and time commitments were too much for them. Most schemes are started by forming a self build housing association and applying for finance from the Housing Corporation. The group, who must select themselves, will register an association with the Registrar of Friendly Societies. Land must then be found, schemes costed and proved feasible before submitting an application for funding to the Corporation. Individual mortgages must also be obtained to purchase the properties after they have been completed (Ospina, 1988). The practical success of the enterprise rests on members spending a considerable part of their leisure time each week on building activites, having sufficient building trade experience, and being exceptionally organized, effective and hard working. The Housing Corporation has continued its support for self build groups and in 1989 helped to set up the Community Self Build Agency. There are also a number of independent consultants who will offer guidance through the whole process.

6.5.2 Secondary co-ops

Many of the people involved in co-ops have limited knowledge of how to obtain finance, develop a scheme and manage it. The Morleys feared the commitment necessary and would have benefited from discussion with the staff of a Secondary Co-op (NFHC undated). This is an organization offering a range of services from assistance with development and setting up the co-op to providing education, training and legal advice. They do not own or occupy property, but may be owned or controlled by primary co-ops. A number are supported by grants. In 1987 there were 14 secondary co-ops distributed in London and the Home Counties, Merseyside, Lancashire and Yorkshire (NFHC, 1987). Education is at the heart of the secondary co-op's work. 'Co-operators are not born; they have, at considerable expense in time and energy, to be made' (Birchall, 1988). All this work may, on occasion, be undertaken by housing associations.

General comment on co-ops

Although there has been support for co-ops from all political parties for different reasons the numbers established have been low. Glasgow Council in the early eighties sought to introduce a community ownership programme by setting up par value co-ops with authority funding. This was a way of circumventing the Conservative government's restrictive financial measures. The Scottish Office was not in favour of the authority promoting co-ops, and the few co-ops which persisted were forced to approach the Housing Corporation for funding. 'In the end, the pressures in favour of the par value co-ops have proved too great, and the Scottish Office has allowed the second stage co-ops to go ahead under the auspices of the Glasgow council' (Ospina, 1987). In the late seventies in Liverpool primary co-ops were helped by two secondary co-ops, the Neighbourhood Housing Services Ltd and the Co-operative Development Services (CDS). The latter worked with families whose homes were being cleared to create a new build co-op, with the families influencing the design. The Weller Street Co-op attained some fame, and its struggles against the professionalism and bureaucracy of CDS, the Housing Corporation and the council, has been described in the book 'the Weller Way' (McDonald, 1986). The way was paved for a second co-op, the Hesketh Street Housing Co-operative where 'there seems little evidence of the primary/secondary conflict recorded in the Weller experience' (Ospina, 1987). A useful appraisal of this scheme is available in the Architects Journal (July 1984). The venture into participatory design was educative and showed the possibilities and difficulties of spreading the method to conventional building schemes.

The present Conservative government is committed to co-op provision and the NFHC sees its smallest sector of housing becoming recognized as a popular and effective form of tenure. Through the 'Tenants' Choice' provision of the Housing Act 1988, tenants are putting themselves forward as their own land-lords and owners. The degree of control over their own housing will be high. It is arguable as to whether this is because co-operation is seen as the way to greater participation or is the best method to improve services and avoid rent rises. Whatever the reason co-ops seem to have a brighter future although it will depend on available financial resources.

6.6 Avenues for participation in housing associations

There is an unfortunate tendency for people in need to be defined as unable to sort out their lives or contribute anything useful to the running of their housing. Research conducted by Platt *et al.* (1987) on behalf of the NFHA and an account of council initiatives in the 1980s (Bartram, undated) found that this was far from the truth. Tenants in both sectors are involved in suc-cessful participatory exercises, serving on the committees of Associations and Housing Committees and running Management Co-ops. The potential benefits of involving tenants are considerable. These include:

- better designed and constructed homes, with longer periods of satisfactory use;
- lower maintenance and repair costs;
- more efficient and responsive housing management and repairs service;
- lower rent arrears;
- greater job satisfaction for staff and lower turnover;
- less duplication of work with tenants, more tenant satisfaction leading to greater pride in and care of the local environment;
- fewer empty properties and quicker re-lettings;
- increased self-confidence amongst tenants, leading to other community de-velopment benefits (LHG, 1989).

There are, of course, difficulties when initiating schemes to involve ten-ants. Housing and management committees have to be persuaded that it is a wise policy and tenants may have to be motivated to take an interest in par-ticipation. It is not a cheap option in that extra costs flow from the changes. However, in the long run decisions will be more effective and may be speeded up. It will be necessary to:

- organize training for staff and tenants;
- give financial support for tenant associations;
- create time for consultation, and restructure departments;
- give financial recognition for the increased role of staff. — liason officers.

The most common chances of participation by tenants in an association are in the following ways:

- in design at a pre-allocation of tenancy;
- through a tenants' association;
- sitting on the management committee;
- running a management co-operative.

It is proposed to examine the Morley's progress through these stages.

6.6.1 Pre-allocation participation

The Association to which the Morleys were nominated had decided to pre-allocate tenancies in a small housing development. This decision was part of their overall policy to involve tenants and applicants wherever possible. There are increased management costs because the amount of staff time taken to implement the policy can be considerable. This increased cost will depend on whether the tenants actively participate in designing the scheme and choose their home, or are allocated a home, and have some limited say about bathroom and kitchen fittings, colour of paint and type of doors, etc.

The Morleys were offered a house, in principle, by the lettings section of the Association. They then had the opportunity of examining the plans and layout of the development, and chose which house they would like. The choice will diminish the lower down the offer list that a family is placed, unless there is allocation by group discussion or draw. The lettings section then notified the development staff of the name and addresses of the prospective tenants.

It is the job of the development staff to discuss and, if necessary, advise tenants on the possible design choices. From the landlord's point of view this is time consuming work and there is a likelihood of people changing their minds, not liking what is on offer and angling for other choices. They will also, understandably, get distressed when there are delays on contracts. However, there is the opportunity for the landlord to explain about the type of systems installed, the benefits and drawbacks of different types of fittings, and generally enlarge the tenants knowledge about property maintenance. This can pay dividends at a later date. For the tenants there is satisfaction in having had an element of choice in both the design and location of their home. In the Morley's case the seed of real participation was also sown.

If the Morleys had participated from the inception of a scheme, they would have worked with the architect on the general design. Most of the information about tenants being involved in design comes from the co-operative world. McDonald's book (1986) on the Weller Street Co-op describes how tenants were led through the intricacies of design choice, and also how tenants tried to educate architects in what they wanted. They developed a common language with the architects through trips to housing schemes and places like the Building Centre, slide shows and discussions, and examining published examples of layout and built schemes. Having established a basic understanding

Table 6.2 The process of participation in design

Design stages	Decision makers
Concept of the scheme	Clients and professionals
Design of the layout	Clients and professionals
Internal design of homes	Individual and professionals
Building the scheme	Tenants' Clerk of Works
Completion	Tenants' Clerk of Works
Allocation processes	As tenants see fit
Management	Tenants or employed help

they made primary decisions on such matters as space standards, cost limits, car parking facilities, variation of home by individual families and how the site might affect the local neighbourhood. This has to be done in the tenants' spare time and architects must be prepared for meetings at all sorts of hours. It is also important to ensure that communcation between tenants and architects is good:

• there must be small weekly meetings of groups and tenant surgeries;
• there should be questionnaires and small group meetings to match design to tenant preferences;
• sketch proposals must be discussed and the final plans agreed;
• allocation of homes can take place by mutual agreement of tenants or a draw;
• tenants manage the scheme.

Table 6.2 sets out the principal steps in the process.

A case study of Hesketh co-op in Liverpool (Architects Journal, 1984) also describes the sort of work involved.

There is no reason why this process could not be transplanted to housing association new building or self-management co-ops, or any remaining future local authority work. The major drawback would be the increased costs of participation which would have to be reflected in higher rents. To counter balance this tenants could agree to cheaper options in the scheme. At the moment tenants have to take what they are given. Under this alternative arrangement they would have a measure of control over what might have to be eliminated to keep cost under control.

It is recognized that such pre-allocation of tenancies is not a widespread activity. The evidence points to it being a worthwhile approach. Full design participation will not always be possible but there is no reason for the 'limited choice' option of equipment and colour schemes not to be offered.

6.6.2 Tenants' Association (TA)

'Standards for Housing Management' (NFHA, 1987) advises housing associations to encourage the formation of tenants' associations, the objective being to have representatives who can speak for all tenants. However, this is no easy matter. People first need to be persuaded of the value of a tenant's association, so a clear and concrete statement of advantages is essential. Properties may be scattered and tenants have little contact with one another. Housing associations often try to stimulate the interest of tenants by calling a public meeting, but frequently this is met with apparent indifference, whilst written material rarely seems to capture tenants' interest. Social events may create a climate for discussions to take place and an embryo group form, but thought must be given to the right setting. Research by Platt *et al.* (1987) suggests that the best way to contact tenants is individually. In a sense Ann Morley was recruited individually at the time of the pre-allocation consultation. Her interest was further stimulated at the time of the 6 month 'snagging'* visit, when she realized that despite careful design discussions, faults still occurred. She saw the value of tenant comment and felt that tenants should continue to contribute to the design of future rehabilitation and new-build schemes. She, therefore, became the prime mover in starting a TA, by canvassing from the group originally housed together. They recruited other tenants and the whole group approached the Housing Association (HA) for discussions about representation on the management committee and practical help in forming a TA.

This stage of a TA's life is crucial. A formal commitment was given by the housing association to the TA in terms of regular meetings with them, methods by which their influence would be recognized and support in the form of finance, training and a place to meet. A sum was set aside in the housing association's budget each year to be used for small capital items like typewriters and filing cabinets. Running costs like printing, photocopying and translating was partly paid for by the Housing Association, partly by fund-raising by the TA and a tenant levy. Distribution of material was undertaken by the housing association through its regular mailings. A senior member of staff or a committee member was designated to take responsibilty for encouraging the TA. In return the tenants made it clear who they were representing and established rules and accountability for financial matters. One of the major activities of the TA was to keep tenants informed, which

---

* Snagging is a jargon term, meaning the inspection of a newly built home, which is carried out 6 months after the home has been completed.

they did through a community newsletter. The TA had access to a community resource centre which had microcomputers and a package for desk-top publishing which made setting up a newsletter easier. The HA also sent a few tenants on a training course.

The Morley's TA was relatively successful and is in line with research by Platt *et al.* (1987) which suggested that three factors may account for a successful TA:

- a housing association invests time and money and is persistent in promoting and supporting the TAs;
- a committee member has taken responsibility for working with the tenants;
- the TA includes residents from outside the Housing Association, so that it is community based rather than just an action group. The fostering of TAs is a long term commitment and must be a step-by-step process.

Some local authorities employ full-time tenant support workers whose task is to assist in the setting up of TAs, Greenwich is an example. Their work includes help to book rooms, invitations to officers and members to meetings, informing groups of committee dates, links with other organizations, printing, photocopying, etc. (Bartram, undated). There is no reason why the bigger housing associations should not create similar posts, or smaller associations combine to pay a peripatetic worker.

6.6.3 Tenants on housing associations committees

Tenants who sit on management committees are in a position to make a substantial contribution to the running of the organization as well as putting the tenants point of view. Ann Morley did not act in a representative capacity but was able to contribute useful ideas.

A survey of management committees (Crook, 1985) found that only 25% of associations had tenants on their committees. The Glasgow University survey (1989) found the same, adding that small associations were likely to give voting rights on the main committee, and the national associations on their local sub-committees. There would also be representation on advisory committees or working parties reporting to the management committee.

All tenants may become members of their own housing association and thereby gain the right to vote for the management committee. Tenants themselves may arrive on a management committee in three ways as:

- an elected TA representative being co-opted onto the committee;
- an elected TA representative standing for election to the committee in their own right at the annual general meeting of the Housing Asociation;
- an individual member co-opted or voted onto the management committee.

When a TA representative is elected the role is clearly defined as representing tenant interests and all matters can be raised. But when an individual tenant is elected or co-opted other committee members are often unsure of the tenants' remit. Such individuals frequently felt themselves under pressure to adopt only broad policy perspectives and not raise individual tenant's problems. The research by Platt *et al.* (1987) found that where representation was through a TA rather than individual membership, tenants felt that they were in a better bargaining position.

A quote by an individual tenant member from that research exemplifies the dilemma. 'There is no clear definition of our role. We are not elected by any tenant body or delegated in anyway, so we are there as individuals, but I behaved as if I was speaking for other tenants'. Some associations allow tenants other than committee members to contribute to discussions concerning their own homes, which may obviate the problem.

Once tenants are elected or invited onto committees, the problem of fitting into the committee arises. It is one of the problems every new member has to face, but there are particular difficulties for a tenant member. Even someone like Sarah Morley, who had some experience, will need support and introduction into the workings of the organization. Committee membership is predominantly white, male, middle class and professional, and can be an intimidating group for inexperienced members. An invitation to meet staff and a few members of the management committee prior to their first formal meeting can help to overcome fear of the unknown. It is also a help if more than one committee place is available to tenants, as there can be mutual support and help. An induction pack is a necessity, as is the offer of attendance at basic training courses. An understanding of the jargon is a major barrier to communication, so that care must be taken to explain terms and housing shorthand. If the association has sub-committees, the new member should be asked their area of interest and appointed to the relevant sub-committee. Staff should ensure that the member has recent 'minutes' and is aware of current issues. Staff attitudes are important, as many tenants feel awkward about facing staff who they see, at other times, in a landlord capacity. These are a few of the basic requirements to enable tenants to become effective committee members. The benefits of participation at committee level are best summarized as;

- helping community development;
- leading to better housing management;
- creating more choice or power for tenants;
- leading to greater tenant satisfaction;
- helping councillors and committee members to do their job (IOH/TPAS, 1989).

6.6.4 Tenant Management Co-ops (TMCs)

The final step in tenant involvement for the Morleys was joining a Tenant Management Co-op. This is an organization formed by the tenants of a housing association or a council to take over some of the housing management functions and maintenance tasks normally carried out by the landlord. The study of co-operative housing in England and Wales (McCafferty and Riley, 1989) found that there were 103 management co-ops in authorities, 99 in housing associations and 99 in other forms of tenure, representing 22% of the total of all co-ops. The majority are in London, with smaller numbers spread around the regions with the exception of Wales. The majority of association co-ops house less than 50 persons by contrast to authorities where the majority house over 100. The small housing development where the Morleys lived typified the sort of scheme which might suit a TMC.

It has been possible to create TMCs since the Housing Rents and Subsidies Act 1975, which was modified by the Housing Acts of 1980 and 1985. Further impetus was given by the Housing and Planning Act 1986 which incorporated significant changes, mainly directed at giving local authority tenants the chance to become managers or owners. Money (under section 16 of the Act) is available to all tenant groups to receive advice and assistance in the formation of TMCs. Similarly, promotion grants are available under the Housing Act 1985 (s87) (as amended by the Housing Act 1988) from the Housing Corporation for management and ownership co-ops.

The reasons for tenants starting a TMC are most likely to be a wish to deliver a better service than the landlord does and to gain control over their housing. The Morleys, having successfully participated in the design of their home and started a TA, felt that a TMC would be a logical next step. As a tenant committee member, Ann had participated in discussions about consultation and improved service delivery. She was therefore well placed to initiate a feasibility study, which is the first step in setting up a TMC. It is essential to have sufficient support from tenants in a delineated number of homes. This means ensuring that the prospective co-operators fully understand what a co-op is, and what participating in it involves.

The steps involved were:

- examining the state of the property and making a decision about the extent of the landlord's liability for repair before the properties were handed over;
- drafting a constitution which met the requirements of the Industrial and Provident Societies Act 1965. This is submitted to the Registrar of the Friendly Societies for approval and registration. (The NFHC offers a model constitution);
- negotiating a Management Agreement between the co-op and the landlord. Such a document sets out the identities of the parties involved, their legal and management responsibilities.

The Morley's TMC took on responsibility for day-to-day repairs, cyclical maintenance, caretaking and cleaning, allocations and lettings, collection of rents and arrears, and landscaping and gardening. It received the same amount of money as the landlord would have expected to spend on the same tasks. The advantage to the tenants is the freedom to make their own spending priorities (Baugh, 1988). Other advantages that accrue to co-ops according to a survey of local authority co-ops (Downey *et al.*, 1982) are:

* tenancy conditions reflecting the preferences of the tenants;
* control over the selection of new members;
* an efficient system of repairs;
* control over their own finances, improved planning of expenditure and surpluses spent as the co-op decided;
* a socially satisfying organization.

Tenants who have established a management co-op in an association have an additional advantage in that they cannot be approached by another landlord (Fraser, 1988).

Interestingly, McCafferty and Riley's (1989) survey of co-operative housing found that housing association management co-ops were least likely to be satisfied with certain aspects of their housing, in comparison to other co-ops. These included the sense of community, the way the communal areas were kept, satisfaction with caretakers, and consultation by the co-op committee. It is difficult to explain these negative findings. Housing association co-ops tended to cater predominantly for families with children, with the head of the household in employment. Perhaps the limited amount of time committee members could spare led to the poor and ineffective management identified in the survey. Despite these comments, the majority of the case study co-ops in this survey 'felt they had succeeded in fulfilling their original objectives and most of the remainder said that whilst they had not achieved their aims in full, they had nevertheless been partially successful' (1989). The study as a whole showed that co-ops were providing 'a small-scale, personalised, locally-based and effective housing service at a competitive cost.'

Tenant control seems to be an area of increasing importance. People like the Morleys will be needed to make such a policy successful, and must be sustained by good advice and assistance. For tenants to run their housing over a long period of years means a commitment which many will not be willing to give. There needs to be a turnover of co-op members to replace those committee members who wish to retire. There also needs to be a psychological climate promoting co-operative housing for the real purpose of tenant control. The question must be asked 'just how committed are people to mutual co-operation as opposed to market competition or bureaucratic control?' (Birchall, 1988). The research so far suggests that this form of housing is truly successful only for those with a strong commitment to the principle of mutual co-operation. The picture may change with financial policies geared to making public landlordism unattractive.

Conclusions

This chapter in looking at the law relating to participation has found that many organizations are not fulfilling their legal obligations. There is little or no participation or consultation at the waiting list stage when applicants must conform to the rules and regulations set out by housing organizations. A proper system of appeal would be of particular value at this stage as the inadequate dissemination of information means that applicants cannot make sensible choices. Even where homelessness is concerned the avenues for appeal are minimal.

The alternatives open to families and individuals on low incomes are limited. The choice is between renting from local authorities and housing associations or trying to find some form of low cost ownership. The chances of the latter will depend on which part of the country you live in and lie between shared ownership, ownership co-operatives and self build.

Once applicants become tenants the possibilities of having some influence on their housing increases, for instance via pre-allocation participation in design. This is a valuable learning experience which can be put to good use when a tenant becomes a member of a housing association's management committee or a co-op. Sympathetic housing association policies on participation can do a great deal to smooth the path of tenants involvement.

Currently, associations are being exhorted by the Housing Corporation and the NFHA to increase participation and such activities will be taken into account when monitoring the association. The DOE and Housing Corporation are offering grant-aid to tenants and advice bodies on 'tenant choice' inititiatives, with co-operative housing coming to the fore. This chapter has concentrated on participation in housing associations, but it should not be forgotten that similar exercises are taking place in local authorities.

Conclusion

In the preface two major themes were mentioned. The first was the tension between the organizational principles of the housing service and the experience of the people using it. The examination of the research discussed, shows very clearly that structures and procedures do not always work to the benefit of the customer. Applicants for rehousing are interviewed at a single particularly needful point in their lives. Staff only perceive their immediate need, and act within the blinkered rules of a tightly regulated system. They fail to give adequate consideration to past history and future needs of the individuals. Senior staff happily make strategic plans based on unfocused statistical evidence that simply does not take real account of tenants' requirements. The examination of housing profiles, related to themes, has served to emphasize that first and foremost housing is about peoples' needs and not administrative convenience. Structures and practice should be directed to giving people the best possible service and solutions to their housing problems.

The second theme concerned the inter-relatedness of all aspects of housing despite inherent conflicts. In examining the housing history of individuals it becomes apparent that attempts to meet need by altering policies or practices in one section will have an effect on another. Tracey's efforts to find a home, for example, point out the conflicting policies of the right to buy for tenants and the right of the individual to a home.

The exploration of the research in specific chapters has shown that good practice does exist, in both local authorities and housing associations. However, the evidence points to the fact that tenants are still disatisfied in particular areas such as the repairs and maintenance service, their influence on decision making and the chances for choices on matters concerning their home. Equal opportunity policies and procedures are also lacking in organizations despite pressure from the CRE, DOE and Housing Corporation. Nowhere is this more apparent than in the attempt to meet the needs of the homeless, where black groups and single parent families headed by women form a significant percentage.

It is true that the possibilities of meeting tenants wishes and requirements are circumscribed by the financial situation and often by the political will of the organization, but many organizations are actively seeking solutions. To this end organizational structures are under review in a number of authorities and associations. The complexity of the housing service has over time led to the creation of large multi-functional housing departments. However, in many areas a fragmented housing service split between two or more departments remains. There are drawbacks to both types of organization, which are detrimental to tenants satisfaction with the housing service. Large ones may become remote from tenants whilst the fragmented organization may lead to tenants' chasing from department to department for answers and an incoherent housing policy. The research shows that there is evidence that both types can work and that it is difficult to come to a conclusion on the best model structure.

Fashions in management also come and go. Decentralization of the housing service is the preferred solution of a number of organizations at present, in an effort to bring the service closer to the tenants. The analysis of the impact of decentralization in Chapter 2, which was carried out in 1988 needs to be developed further to take account of new ideas of customer care and service delivery. It is argued that decentralization is no passing fad, such a structure allied with greater opportunities for tenants to increase their say in their affairs, could be successful. The success of an organization is also dependent on the quality of its staff. They are a major resource but, as the research makes clear, there is an overwheming necessity for the training, motivating and nursing of staff. The speed of change may create insecurity and frustration as well as challenge. Managers are learning to manage change.

There is comfort in the Glasgow University (1989) and Welsh Office (1989) research on local authorities and housing associations that there is not much to chose between their quality of management. Both face certain dangers. Firstly, the constant changes in relevant legislation put strain on efficient and sensitive delivery of the housing service. Management energy is often channelled into finding ways around new legislation or government circulars. This means that management reacts to government wishes rather than having time to present plans and strategies designed to improve services. Secondly, the lack of financial resources for both authorities and associations has led to fewer and poorer quality homes being built or rehabilitated, thereby diminishing the service to tenants and applicants. Thirdly, the pressure on staff in organizations where there is insufficient money to fill all the posts has led to an impoverished service and overworked staff. Lastly, it is tempting to cosmetically re-structure as an answer to internal problems rather than constantly reviewing and steadily improving the organization on an incremental basis.

The future of housing management is the concern of tenants, applicants, housing organizations and central government, although all the participants have different agendas. A unifying management practice could be the introduction of Performance Indicators to measure management efficiency and effectiveness. By this method all participants should be able to assess how an organization performs. However, the lack of a qualitative dimension to a number of the indicators limits the usefulness of the exercise but despite this they will be used by the DOE and the Housing Corporation to monitor the management success of an organization. Tenants, however, may like to see performance measured in a different way.

There is also considerable debate about the future of council housing. So far 'tenants choice' has been exercised, in the main, by tenants in favour of local authorities. Tenants may have voted in such a way to stay with 'the devil you know', but improved management practice may also have been a factor. The continuing financial squeeze is forcing rents upwards and narrowing opportunities to improve the housing stock, so there is no guarantee that future votes will be in favour of staying with authorities. Arguments to set up local authority associations, in order to obtain capital monies for investment, are seductive. If tenants are asked to vote for such a change they will have an unprecendented opportunity to bargain for a service standard that meets their wishes.

Whether council housing continues in its present form or associations change in character, the need for imaginative housing management will not diminish. The housing service, in its broadest sense of management, development to meet new and changing needs and the improvement of public and private sector stock will always have to look at housing for the life of many citizens and try to achieve that goal by good housing management practice.

Appendix A Example of a tenancy agreement

NOTTINGHAM CITY COUNCIL

DEPARTMENT OF HOUSING SERVICES

TENANCY AGREEMENT FOR COUNCIL DWELLING

THE AGREEMENT This is the Tenancy Agreement which sets out your responsibilities as a tenant and the Council's responsibilities as your Landlord, such as the repair and decoration of the premises, the payment of rent and the circumstances in which your tenancy can be brought to an end.
You will find further explanations of your rights in your Tenant's Handbook. **You are advised to read this Agreement carefully before signing it.**

FULL NAME OF TENANT/TENANTS This is a Tenancy Agreement between Nottingham City Council

('the Council')

AND

_____

_____ ('the tenant')

ADDRESS OF PREMISES _____

_____

_____ ('the premises')

COMMENCEMENT OF TENANCY _____

DECLARATION I agree to accept the tenancy of the above addressed premises on the terms and conditions set out in this agreement. I acknowledge the receipt of .... keys for the dwelling and agree to return all the keys at the end of the tenancy. I also acknowledge the receipt of a copy of this agreement.

Signatures 1. _____

of tenant(s) 2. _____

Date: _____

Signed on behalf of the Council _____

TENANCY AGREEMENT

WHAT THE TENANT IS RESPONSIBLE FOR:-

(This applies equally to Joint Tenants).

By signing the Tenancy Agreement you have committed yourself to certain responsibilities, these are as follows:-

Rent

A)   You have agreed to pay rent to the City Council on the date the rent is due, including any other charges for the premises that are noted on the Rent Card, for example, Heating, Rates, Water Charges, Service Charges, etc.

B)   The City Council may alter the amount of the Rent but must give to you not less than four weeks written notice. This notice will also tell you of your rights to end the Tenancy if you are not prepared to accept the new Rent level and it also tells you how to end the Tenancy.

Repairs

A)   You will have to carry out at your own expense minor internal repairs all as shown on the list attached to this Tenancy Agreement. There are certain Tenants who do not have to carry out these repairs. These Tenants are noted on the list attached. This list may be altered by the City Council but an up to date copy will always be available for inspection at your Local District or Neighbourhood Office and you may have a copy if you ask for one.

B)   You are responsible for repairing damage to any part of your home caused by the wilful or negligent or careless action of yourself, a member of your household, visitors or friends.

C)   You are also responsible for keeping the internal decoration of your home up to a reasonable standard.

D)   To help the City Council keep your home in good repair you must report promptly to your Local Housing Office any leakages from pipes, defects in fixtures and fittings or structure or any other repair for which the City Council is responsible.

Access

A)   You must allow access to your home to an authorised employee of the City Council or any of the main service Authorities, for example British Gas, East Midlands Electricity, Severn Trent Water Authority, this is provided you have had twenty four hours written notice, and provided the visit is to inspect equipment or to carry out any works which the City Council or the other Organisations think are necessary.

In an Emergency employees of the City Council may enter your home using any means necessary, but upon completion of their work your home will be properly secured and repaired if necessary (an Emergency in these circumstances is when either property or life is at risk).

Nuisance and Harassment

As a responsible Tenant you will be expected to act in a reasonable way towards your home and the people living nearby, in particular you must not act in a way which causes nuisance, disturbance or annoyance to anyone else living nearby. You must not harass people because of their religious beliefs, their sex, their race or anything else. If you do you will have broken the Tenancy Agreement and the City Council may take legal action to end the Tenancy.

Visitors to your Home As the Tenant you are responsible for actions of any visitors or relatives which break this Tenancy Agreement.

Use of your Home You have agreed by signing the Tenancy Agreement to use your home only for a private dwelling and for no other purpose.

The Garden
(where provided) You will be expected to keep tidy and neat all garden areas and hedges to the reasonable satisfaction of the City Council. This is to prevent annoyance to neighbours and danger to other persons.

Changes and
Alterations On signing this Agreement you have accepted that you will obtain the City Council's written permission **Before** you do any of the following:-

1) Exchanging or signing over the Tenancy with or to another person, including a member of your family or household.

2) Letting part or the whole of your home to anyone.

3) Carrying out alterations or adaptations to the property (**please note:** it can be very dangerous to alter the position of walls or to alter fire doors without first having asked for expert advice).

4) Putting up a garage, shed, greenhouse, pigeon loft, fencing or other structure on any part of your home or garden area.

5) Parking a caravan, boat, vehicle, or any other moveable structure in your home or garden.

If you wish to do any of these things, you must apply in writing to the City Council, then either permission will be granted or reasons for refusal will be given. Permission will not be unreasonably withheld.

Lodgers You may take in Lodgers if you wish, but you must first notify your local Housing Office. In normal circumstances it will be your decision whether or not to take in Lodgers but the City Council will object if overcrowding results.

Flats and
Maisonettes If you are the Tenant of a City Council Flat or Maisonette you have special responsibilities because of the design of your home and those of your neighbours, as follows:-

A) You must not place or leave objects on the common corridors, walkways or balconies.

B) You must not place or leave vehicles in the forecourts, service roads, parking areas adjoining the flat complex in such a way as to obstruct the free passage of emergency vehicles or other Tenants and visitors.

C) You must not erect an outdoor Wireless, Television, Short/Long Wave Radio Aerial or Satellite Dish without written permission from the City Council.

D) You must use the rubbish chutes for getting rid of small items of rubbish but take particular care not to block the chutes or cause a fire in them. Large items of rubbish must not be put down the rubbish chute but can be collected if you arrange this with the caretaker.

E) **The keeping of Cats and Dogs in Flats and Maisonettes is not allowed.** You may only keep small Pets such as Birds which live in Cages.

F) **For Safety and Health Reasons** you must not use or store in your home bottled Gas or Paraffin appliances or any other inflammable liquids or substances, for example, Petrol, Oil, etc.

Ending Your Tenancy

When you decide to end your Tenancy you must:-

1) Notify the Housing Department, in writing four weeks before you move out of your home.
2) Return all keys to the Housing Department.
3) Leave the home and garden clean and tidy: clear of **all belongings**
4) Leave the City Council's fixtures and fittings in the same state as they were when your Tenancy began, except for wear and tear, unless of course, you have provided similar items to a standard acceptable to the Housing Department. All these items must be left behind when you leave.
5) Pay the City Council on demand the cost of clearing rubbish or repairs which result from your neglect.

WARNING TO TENANTS WHO HAVE GAS FIRES & SOLID FUEL (SMOKELESS FUEL) FIRES:-

For your own safety you should check any Flue or Chimney connected to any heating appliance **at least once a year** and keep it free from obstruction. In most cases this can be done by having your Chimneys swept but if you need further advice, please contact your Local Housing Office.

LANDLORD AND TENANT ACT 1987, SECTION 48

'The Landlord and Tenant Act 1987 now means that the City Council has to notify you formally where you can serve Notices (including Notices of Proceedings) on the City Council your Landlord. If you should need to serve such Notices, please send them to **The City Secretary at the Guildhall, Nottingham, NG1 4BT'**.

Help and Advice

The City Council through all its Departments, but in particular through the Housing Services Department, will provide advice and assistance on all Housing matters.

If you have any problems associated with Housing and your home you should contact your Local District or Neighbourhood Office. If your enquiries are about Rents, Rebates, Housing Benefit or other Housing Charges you should contact **the City Treasurer's Department.**

Your elected **Ward Councillor** is able to give advice and assistance.

Consultation

The City Council will consult with secure Tenants on Housing matters which affect them. (A secure Tenancy is the normal City Council Tenancy).

Insurance

Although you cannot be required to insure the contents of your home it is very sensible to do so, particularly if you live in a Flat or Maisonette.
The City Council has arranged with a well known Insurance Company a very reasonably priced Insurance package and you are strongly advised to take advantage of the arrangement.

Appendix B
Basic procedures for jobbing repairs

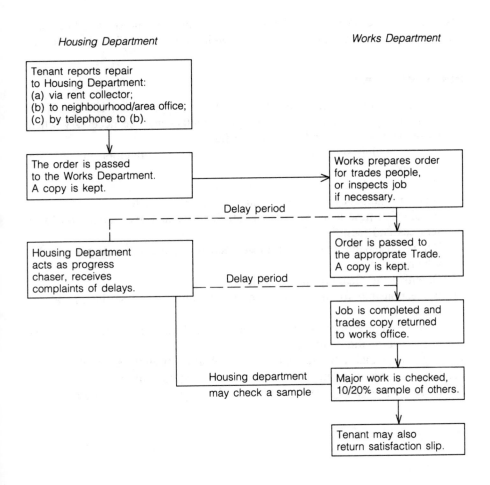

Housing Department

Works Department

Tenant reports repair
to Housing Department:
(a) via rent collector;
(b) to neighbourhood/area office;
(c) by telephone to (b).

The order is passed
to the Works Department.
A copy is kept.

Works prepares order
for trades people,
or inspects job
if necessary.

Delay period

Housing Department
acts as progress
chaser, receives
complaints of delays.

Order is passed to
the approprate Trade.
A copy is kept.

Delay period

Job is completed and
trades copy returned
to works office.

Housing department
may check a sample

Major work is checked,
10/20% sample of others.

Tenant may also
return satisfaction slip.

Appendix C
Warden's job description

General

The Warden is responsible for the day-to-day running of the sheltered housing scheme and for giving support to tenants whilst fostering their independence.

Range of duties

1. To make daily contact with every resident by personal visit or via an intercom speech system. More frequent contact may be necessary when individuals are sick or have become frail.
2. Provide a link support with relatives, neighbours, doctors and welfare services.
3. Ensure that all residents know how to use the intercom system.
4. Answer emergency calls and summon appropriate help.
5. Ensure that new tenants settle in satisfactorily and give advice on local services and facilities.
6. Report all tenants repairs and those needed in the communal parts of the scheme.
7. Organize the cleaning of the building.
8. Be responsible for the security of the building and test the fire alarm regularly.
9. Control the use of the communal laundry and help and instruct residents in the use of the equipment.
10. Organize social activities and foster a pleasant friendly atmosphere.
11. Keep records in relation to residents, staff, equipment, etc.
12. Liaise with housing office staff or Senior Warden as appropriate.

Appendix D
Factors used in points schemes

The following range of factors are used in local authority and housing association points schemes. Points are awarded to individual factors and will be weighted to ensure that applicants experiencing the most need rise to the top of the list. Weighting can of course be manipulated to ensure that particular approved groups gain the most points. Schemes can only be considered to be partially objective but are preferable to individual merit and date order schemes.

1. Medical reasons
   Priority A — Where rehousing is seen to be the only solution, e.g. physical disability or degenerative illness.
   Priority B — has a medical condition which may get a lot worse unless rehousing is offered.
2. Housing insecurity
   Group A — homeless.
   Group B — not likely to become homeless but is, say, experiencing friction in the family.
   Group C — if there is no legal right to a tenancy, e.g. a lodger or informal tenant.
3. Social need
   Points are given for a range of social situations and the ability to cope with the situation will be assessed. The need may be one or more of the following:
   violence or fear of it;

harassment because of race, sex, religion or from a neighbour or landlord;
relationship breakdown;
bereavement;
separated families;
applicants needing to live near relatives to receive or give support.
4. Property condition
   A range of points may be given reflecting the severity of the condition.
5. Overcrowding
   Points are given for lack of bedroom space based on a standard which
   assumes that a separate bedroom is needed for:
   a couple;
   the parent of a single family;
   a person over 16 years old;
   each other person over 10 years unless they share with someone of the
   same sex.
6. Sharing facilities or lacking them
   Points are awarded for the lack of facilities which will include, sink,
   inside toilet, bath, separate kitchen.
7. Multiple occupation
   Applicants will qualify for points if they occupy a hostel, hotel, bed-and-
   breakfast accommodation or other house in multiple occupation.
8. Children under 16 years old living above ground floor.
9. Elderly applicants over 75 years living in unsuitable accommodation,
   e.g. excessive stairs.
10. Under-occupation
    Points will be given for spare number of bedrooms.
11. Families living in caravans.
12. Points may be given for the length of time on the waiting list.

Few schemes will include all the above factors they will be tailored to the
needs of an area. For example, multiple occupation rarely occurs in a rural
area.

References

Abrahams, C. and Mungall, R. (1989) *Housing Vulnerable Young People. NCH*, Young Runaways Project.

Allport, G. (1954) *The Nature of Prejudice*, Addison Wesley.

Architects Journal (18.7.84) *Co-op Dirvdends* (an appraisal of the Hesketh Street Scheme by a group of involved professionals and co-op members).

Ash, J. (1982) Tenant Participation. Part II. Requirements of Techniques, *Housing Review*, **31** (4), 138–140.

Ash, J. (1982a) Tenant Participation. Part I. A Review of Techniques, *Housing Review* **31** (2), 55–57.

Association of Metropolitan Authorities (1985) *Housing and Race: Policy and Practice in Local Authorities*, AMA.

Association of Metropolitan Authorities (1987a) *Homes Above All*. Greater London Houses in Multiple Occupation Survey, AMA.

Association of Metropolitan Authorities (1987) *Multiple Occupation a Time for Action*, AMA.

Association of Metropolitan Authorities (1988) *A Good Practice Guide to Housing Repairing for the Future*, AMA.

Audit Commission (1984) *Bringing Council Tenants' Arrears under Control*, HMSO.

Audit Commission (1985) *Good Management in Local Government Successful Practice and Action*, Local Training Board.

Audit Commission (1986) *Managing the Crisis in Council Housing*, HMSO.

Audit Commission (1989) *Housing the Homeless. The Local Authority Role*, HMSO.

Audit Commission (1989) *Survey of Local Authority Rent Arrears*, HMSO.

Bains Report (1972) *The new local authorities, management and structure*, DOE.

Bartram, M. (undated) *Consulting Tenants. Council Initiatives in the Late 1980s*, Community Rights Project.

Baugh, G. (1988) Setting up a Management Co-op, *Roof*, May/June, pp. 38–41.

Berthoud, R. and Casey, B. (1988) *The Cost of Care in Hostels*, Policy Studies Institute.

Beuret, K. and Stoker, G. (Autumn, 1986) The Labour Party and neighbourhood decentralisation: flirtation or commitment? *Critical Social Policy*, Longman, pp. 4–22.

Birchall, J. (1988) *Building Communities the Co-operative Way*, Routledge and Kegan Paul.

Blunkett, D. and Green, G. (1983) *Building from the Bottom: The Sheffield experience*, Fabian Tract No. 491.

Boddy, M. and Fudge, C. (1984) *Local Socialism*, Macmillan.

Boys, J. (1984) *Women and Public Space*, In Matrix, Making Space: Women in the Man-made Environment, Pluto.

Brailey, M. (1986) *Womens' Access to Council Housing*, Glasgow Planning Exchange Occasional Paper 25.

Bramley, G., Doogan, K., Leather, P., Murie, A. and Watson, E. (1988) *The London Housing Market*, School for Advanced Studies, Occasional Paper, 32.

Bright, J. and Petterson, G. (1984) *The Safe Neighbourhood Unit*, NACRO.

Brion, M. and Davies, C. (1984) *Equal Opportunities for Women*, In Labour Housing Group *Right to a Home* Spokesman.

Brown, C. (1984) *Black and White Britain*, Heinemann.

Building Societies Association (1983) *Housing Tenure*, London Building Society Association.

Burney, E. (1967) *Housing on Trial*, Oxford University Press.

Butler, A., Oldham, C. and Greve, J. (1983) *Sheltered Housing for the Elderly*, Allen and Unwin.

Campaign Bedsit Rights (1989) *Bedsit Rights. A Handbook for people who live in bedsits, flatlets, shared houses, lodgings hostels, bed and breakfast hotels.*

Caring for People. Community Care in the next decade and beyond (1989) White Paper Cmnd. 849 HMSO.

Central Statistical Office (1988) *Social Trends 18*, Table 4.6, HMSO.

City University, Housing Research Group (1978) *Local Housing Management in Manchester*, City University, London.

City University, Housing Research Group (1981) *Could Local Authorities be Better Landlords?* City University.

Clapham, D. (Winter, 1985/86) Management of the Local State, the Example of Corporate Planning, *Critical Social Policy*, Longman.

Clapham, D. and English, J. (Eds) (1987) *Public Housing: Current trends and future developments*, Croom Helm.

Clapham, D. and Kintrea, K. (1986) The social consequences of the allocation process: evidence from Glasgow, *Housing Review*, **35** (3), May–June.

Clapham, D. and Kintrea, K. (1987) Importing Housing Policy: Housing Co-operatives in Britain and Scandanavia, *Housing Studies*, **2** (3), 157–69.

Cole, I., Windle, K. and Arnold, P. (1988) *Understanding Decentralisation*, PAVIC Sheffield City Polytechnic.

Cole, I., Arnold, P. and Windle, K. (1988) *Decentralisation — The Views of Elected Members*, Research Working Paper No 4, Sheffield City Polytechnic.

Commission for Racial Equality (1984) *Race and Council Housing in Hackney,* Report of a formal investigation, CRE.

Commission for Racial Equality (1989) *Racial Discriminination in Liverpool City Council.*

Commission for Racial Equality (1989) *Training for Racial Equality in Housing.*

Commission for Racial Equality (1991) *Race Relations Code of Practice in Rented Housing*, Commission for Racial Equality, London.

Community Development Housing Group (1986) *But, Will it Fly Mr Wright?* TPAS Glasgow.

Community Rights Project and Community Advisory Group (1987) In *Decisions 6. Tenant Participation in Housing*, CRP/CAG.

Cope, H. (1990) *Housing Associations. Policy and practice*, Macmillan.

Craddock, J. (1975) *Council Tenants — Their participation in housing management*, Association of London Boroughs.

Crook, T. (1985) Committees and their members, *Voluntary Housing*, **17**(6), 29–32.

Cullingworth Committee (1969) *Council Housing, Purposes, Procedures and Priorities,* of the Housing Management sub-committee, 9th Report. Central Housing Advisory Committee. HMSO.

Daniel, W. W. (1968) *Racial Discrimination in England*, Penguin.

Darley, G. (1989) *Octavia Hill*, Constable.

Dennis, N. (1972) *Public Participation and Planners Blight*, Faber and Faber.

Department of the Environment *Wheelchair and Mobility Housing: Standards and costs.* Circular 92/75. DOE. 163/75 WO.

Department of the Environment (1979) *National Dwelling and Housing Survey*, HMSO.

Department of the Environment (1983) (Ritchie, J., Keegan, J. and Bosanquet, N.) *Housing for Mentally Ill and Mentally Handicapped People.*

Department of the Environment (1985) *New Homes From Old, Urban Housing Renewal Unit*, DOE, D45AR.

Department of the Environment (1988) *Responding to Homelessness: Local Authority Policy and Practice*, HMSO.

Department of the Environment (1989a) *The Government's Review of the Homelessness Legislation*, DOE.

Department of the Environment (Circular 82/69, WO. 84/69), *Housing Standards and Costs: Accommodation Specially Designed for Old People*, HMSO.

Department of the Environment (Circular 19/90) *S167 (1), Local Government and Housing Act 1989. Housing Management Performance Indicators*, DOE, HMSO.

Department of the Environment (Oct., 1989) *Performance Indicators for Local Authority Tenants*, Consultation Paper, DOE.

Department of the Environment (Revised, 1987) *Shared Ownership. How to become a home-owner in stages*, DOE, HMSO.

Department of the Environment. (Circular 8/76, WO 15/76). *Housing Co-operatives.*

Department of the Environment. Housing (Homeless Persons) Act (1977). *Code of Guidance England and Wales.* DOE/DHSS/WO (Revised, 1983).

Dibblin, J. (1989) *Waving or Drowning Roof*, May/June, pp. 18–21.

Downey, P., Matthews, A. and Mason, S. (1982) *Management Co-operatives. Tenant Responsibility in Practice*, HMSO.

Drucker, P. E. (1965) *The Practice of Management*, Pan Books, London.

Duncan, S. and Kirby, K. (1983) *Preventing Rent Arrears*, HMSO.

Dutta, R. and Taylor, G. (1989) *Housing Equality: An action guide,* CHAR, London.

Dwelly, T. (1990) *Statue Tory Framework Roof*, Jan/Feb, pp. 27–30.

Ealing Housing Aid (1986) *Homeless in Ealing. The use of temporary accommodation*, EHA.

Eardley, T. (1989) *Move-on Housing. The permanent housing needs of residents of hostels and special needs housing projects in London*, NFHA.

Embury, L. and Silver, S. (1989) Money Trouble, *Housing*, **25** (8), 7–9.

Estate Action (undated) *A Guide to Community Refurbishment Schemes*, DOE.

Evans, A. and Duncan, S. (1988) *Responding to Homelessness. Local Authority Policy and Practice*, DOE, p. 17.

Fair Deal for Housing (1971) Cmnd., 4728 White Paper, HMSO. London.

Fisk, M. (1984) Community Alarm Systems, *Housing Review*, **33** (1), 22–3.

Flett, H. (1981) *Black People and Council Housing*, Gower.

Forbes, D. (1988) *Action on Racial Harassment: Legal remedies and Local Authorities*, Legal Action Group and London Housing Unit.

Fowler, C. B. (1988) *Human Resource Management in Local Government*, Longmans/LGTB, p. 29.

Fraser, R. (1988) *Tipping the Balance. A Guide to 'Tenants' Choice'*, TPAS.

Gallop Omnibus Report (1988) Council Tenants. 30 March–12 April 1988 Social Surveys (Gallop Poll) Ltd For the National Consumer Council.

GLC Housing and Women's Committees (1986) *Women and Housing Policy*, GLC Housing Research and Policy Report No. 3.

Glendinning, R., Allen, P. and Young, H. (1989) *The Sale of Local Authority Housing to the Private Sector*, HMSO.

Goodrich, C. (1986) For a Start ..... and where to go next. *Voluntary Housing*, **18** (7), 14–20.

Goslyn, S. (1988) *Advising Older People. A guide for housing staff*, NFHA and Church Housing Association.

Green, H. (1985) *Informal Carers. General Household Survey*, DHSS.

Greenwood, R. and Stewart, J. D. (1974) *Corporate planning in English Local Government*. C. Knight.

Greves, J. (1986) *Homeless in London*, SAUS, University of Bristol.

Hambledon, R. (1978) *Policy Planning and Local Government*, Hutchinson.

Hambleton, R. and Hoggett (1984) *The Politics of Decentralisation: theory and practice of a radical local government initiative*, Working Paper 46, SAUS.

Hambleton, R. and Hoggett, P. (1987) 'Beyond Bureaucratic Paternalism' in Hoggett P. and Hambleton, R. (Eds) *Decentralisation and Democracy: Localising public services*, SAUS, Bristol.

Hambleton, R., Hoggett, P. and Tolan, F. (1989) The Decentralisation of Public Services: A Research Agenda, *Local Government Studies*, January/February.

Handy, C. B. (1985) (3rd edn) *Understanding Organisations*, Penguin, pp. 197–206.

Harrison, L. and Means, R. (1990) *Housing — the essential element in community care*, SHAC.

Henderson, J. and Karn, V. (1987) *Race, Class and State Housing in Britain*, Gower.

Housing Review Reports of Seminars (July/Aug, 1985 and May/June, 1984) *A better Place to live — improving estates*. Housing Centre Trust.

Housing (NI) Order (1988).

Housing Act (1969).

Housing Act (1974).

Housing Act (1980).

Housing Act (1985).

Housing Act (1988).

Housing Association Weekly (30.3.90, No 159) *£59m for homelessness in South East*, p. 8.

Housing and Planning Act (1986). Sections 10–11.

Housing Association Weekly (1.12.89). Furniture turnaround, No. 144. 20.

Housing Corporation (1989) Performance Expectations.

Housing Corporation (Circular 43/1988) *'The Tenants' Guarantee' Guidance on Housing Management. Practice for assured tenancies.*

Housing Corporation. Circular 48/89, *A Guide to tenant selection, LA nominations and statutory homeless* (replaces 16/80).

Housing Corporation. Circular HCO2/85, *Projects for frail elderly people*, HC, 1985.

Housing: The Government's Proposals. (1987) White Paper. CM214. HMSO.

Housing Review (1984, 1985) Reports of Seminars (May/June 1984, July/Aug 1985). *A Better Place to Live – Improving Estates*, Housing Centre Trust.

Humble, J. (1978) *Management by Objectives*, Gower Press.

Hunt, E. (1986) *Sheltered Housing for Frail Elderly*, Housing Review, **35** (4), 135–136.

Inside Housing (8.12.89) **6** (48), p. 5.

Inside Housing (19.1.90). **7** (3), p. 1.

Inside Housing (18.5.90) **7** (19), p. 3.

Inside Housing (8.6.90) **7** (22), p. 4.

Institute of Housing (1988) *Who Will House the Homeless?*

Institute of Housing, Computer Working Party (1984) IOH Survey on impact of new technology, *Housing*, **20** (3), 21–3.

Institute of Housing Working Party (1987) *Preparing for Change.*

Institute of Housing/Tenant Participation Advisory Service (1989) *Tenant Participation in Housing Management*, IOH/TPAS.

Islington Council (1989) (S. Voutsadakis) (2nd edn) *Housing for People with Disabilities: A design guide.*

Kay, A. and Legg, C. (undated) *Tenants' Rights in Practice*, The City University.

Keeble, P. (1983) *Local Authority Provision of Housing Services for Disabled People*, Royal Association for Disability and Rehabilitation.

Kettle, M. and Massie, B. (1986) *Employers' Guide to Disabilities*, Woodhead-Faulkner.

Kirby, K., Finch, H. and Wood, D. (1988) *The Organisation of Housing Management in English Local Authorities*, DOE/HMSO.

Kirkwood, J. (1984) *Information Technology and Land Administration*, The Estates Gazette Ltd.

Labour Housing Group (1990) *Guidelines for Tenant Involvement.*

Levison, D. and Atkins, J. (1987) *The Key to Equality: The 1986 women and housing survey*, Institute of Housing.

Lewis, A. (1989) Getting to the Core, *Voluntary Housing*, **22** (7), 21–24.

Local Government and Housing Act (1989) Section 131.

Local Government Planning and Land Act 1980.

London Borough of Islington (1987) *Going Local: Decentralisation in practice*, Islington Council Press.

London Research Centre (1989) *Private Sector Leasing in London.*

Lord Redcliffe Maud and Wood, B. (1974) *English Government Reformed*, Oxford University Press.

Malpass, P. and Murie, A. (1987) (2nd edn) *Housing Policy and Practice*, Macmillan.

Matrix (1984) *Making Space: Women in the man-made environment*, Pluto.

Matthews, A. (1981) *Management of Co-operatives. The early stages*, HMSO.

Matthews, R. (1983) *Restrictive Practices. Waiting list restrictions and housing need.* Shelter.

McCafferty, P. and Riley, D. (1989) *A Study of Co-operative Housing*, HMSO.

McDonald, A. (1986) *The Weller Way*, Faber and Faber, London.

Ministry of Housing and Local Government (1961) *Homes for Today and Tomorrow* (The Parker Morris Report), HMSO.

Morris, J. and Winn, M. (1990) *Housing and Social Inequality*, Hilary Shipman.

Morton, J. (1982) *Ferndale. A caring repair service for elderly home owners.* Shelter/ Age Concern.

Mullins, L. J. (1989) (2nd edn) *Management and Organisational Behaviour*, Pitman, pp. 72.

Municipal Year Book, (1989) Vol. 2.

NACRO (1988) Crime Prevention Advisory Committee Working Group NACRO.

National Audit Office (1987) *Ministry of Defence and Property Services Agency: Control and management of the defence*, HMSO.

National Federation of Housing Associations/Association of Metropolitan Authorities/ Association of District Councils (1989) *Joint Statement by NFHA, AMA and ADC on local authority nominations to housing associations.*

National Federation of Housing Associations (1982) *Race and Housing: A guide for housing association.*

National Federation of Housing Associations (1983) *Race and Housing: still a cause for concern.*

National Federation of Housing Associations (1984) *Report of Women and Housing Working Party.*

National Federation of Housing Associations (1984) *Transferable Discounts: Home ownership for tenants of charitable associations.*

National Federation of Housing Associations (1985) *Partners or Agents? Housing Associations and Voluntary Agencies.*

National Federation of Housing Associations (1985a) *Ethnic Record Keeping and Monitoring.*

National Federation of Housing Associations (1985b) *The Inquiry into British Housing*, NFHA.

National Federation of Housing Associations (1986) *Housing for Frail Elderly People*, NFHA.

National Federation of Housing Associations (1987) *Standards for Housing Management*, NFHA.

National Federation of Housing Associations (1988) *Self Build. A manual for self build housing associations*, NFHA.

National Federation of Housing Associations (1989) *Race and Housing: Employment and training guide.*

National Federation of Housing Associations (1989a) *Housing Benefit and Income Support for Housing Schemes Providing Care or Support*, 1989/90, NFHA.

National Federation of Housing Co-operatives (1987) Directory, NFHC.

National Federation of Housing Co-operatives and MIND (1989) *Housing the Foundation of Community Care*.

New Earnings Survey Annual Reports.

NFHC Secondary Co-op Group (undated) *Building the Co-operative Future. The role of secondary housing co-ops*.

Niner, P. (1989) *Homelessness in Nine Local Authorities: Case studies of policy and practice*, DOE.

Niner, P. with Karn, V. (1985) *Housing Association Allocations: Achieving racial equality*, The Runnymede Trust.

Office of Population Censuses and Surveys (Martin, J., Meltzer, H. and Elliot, D.) (1988) *The Prevalence of Disability Among Adults* Report No. 1, OPCS Surveys of Disability in Great Britain HMSO (see also subsequent reports in the series).

Ordione, G. S. (1965) *Management by Objectives*, Pitman.

Ospina, J. (1987) *Housing Ourselves*. Shipman. London.

Ospina, J. (1988) Self-building the challenge for Britain. *Housing Review* Mar/April, Housing Centre Trust.

Palmer, C. and Poulton, K. (1987) *Sex and Race Discrimination in Employment*, Legal Action Group.

Penton, J. and Barlow, A. (1980) (2nd edn) *A Handbook of Housing for Disabled People*, The London Housing Consortium West Group.

Peters, T. and Waterman, K. (1982) *In Search of Excellence*, Harper and Row.

Phillips, D. (1986) *What Price Equality?*, GLC Housing Research and Policy Report, No. 9.

Platt, S., Piepe, R. and Smyth, J. (1987) *Heard or Ignored*, NFHA.

Powell, B. (1981) *Walsall's Haul to Democracy*.

Power, A. (1984) *Local Housing Management, A priority estates project survey*. DOE.

Power, A. (1987) *Property Before People. The management of twentieth century housing*, Allen and Unwin.

Power, A. (1987) *The PEP Guide to Local Housing Management Nos 1,2 and 3. Estate Action*, DOE, Welsh Office.

Prescott-Clarke, P., Allen, P. and Morrisey, C. (1988) *Queueing for Housing: A study of council housing waiting lists*, HMSO.

Randolph, B. and Levison, D. (1988) *A Profile of New Tenancies. Preliminary results of the 1988 NFHA census of new lettings*, NFHA.

Rex, J. and Moore, R. (1967) *Race, Community and Conflict*, Oxford University Press.

Rose, E. A. (1982) *Housing Needs and the Elderly*, Gower.

Seabrook, J. (1984) *The Ideal of Neighbourhood*, Pluto Press.

Seex, A. (1987) 'Manchester's Approach to Decentralisation', *Local Government Policy Making*, Vol. 14, No. 2 Sept, 1987.

Sharp, C. (1987) Improving the Public Sector — tenant improvement grants in Sheffield. *Housing Review*, **36** (2), pp. 52–53.

Sheffield Degree Students (1986) Community Alarm Systems. Unpublished Project.

Shelter (1988) *Freedom to Lose: Housing policy and people with disabilities*.

Shelter (1990) (J. Morris) *Our Homes, Our Rights.*

Simpson, A. (1981) *Stacking the Decks: A study of race, inequality and council housing in Nottingham*, Nottingham Community Relations Council.

Skellington, R. (1981) How blacks lose out in council housing, *New Society*, January **29**.

Smith, D. and Whalley, A. (1975) *Racial Minorities and Council Housing*, Political and Economic Planning.

Smith, M. E. (1989) (3rd edn) *Guide to Housing*, Housing Centre Trust.

Social Security Act 1986.

Social Trends (1989) Ch. 8 *Housing*, Central Statistical Service.

Southwark Housing Research and Development (1984) *A Safe Place to Live?*, London Borough of Southwark.

Spicker, P. (1983) *The Allocation of Council Housing*, Shelter.

Stanford, T. (1989) The need to quantify the risks, *Voluntary Housing*, **22** (7), 25–8.

Stanforth, J., Malcolm, J. and Maclennan, D. (1986) *The Delivery of Repair Services in Public Sector Housing in Scotland*. Scottish Office. Central Research Unit Papers.

Stearn, J. (1988) Rights for Rent. *Housing*, **24** (6), 10–13.

Stewart, J. D. (1988) *Understanding the Management of Local Government; Its special purposes, conditions and tasks*, Longman/Local Government Training Board.

Stewart, J. D. (1988) *A new management for housing departments*, Local Government Training Board.

Stewart, J. D. (1971) *Management in Local Government: A viewpoint*, Charles Knight.

Stone, I. (1988) *Equal Opportunities in Local Authorities*, Equal Opportunities Commission.

Thomas, A. and Niner, P. (1989) *Living in Temporary Accommodation. A Survey of homeless people*, DOE, HMSO.

Thorpe, S. (1985) *Housing Design Sheets*, Centre on Environment for the Handicapped.

Tinker, A. (1984) Staying at Home: Helping elderly people. *Housing Review*, **33** (6), 236–238.

Tong, D., Wilson, S. and Ellis, P. (1986) An Introduction to the Information Needs of Housing Management, *Housing Review*, **35** (2), 57–60.

University of Glasgow Centre for Housing Research (1989) *The Nature and Effectiveness of Housing Management in England*, HMSO.

Ware, V. (1988) *Women's Safety on Housing Estates*, Women's Design Service.

Welsh Office (1989) *The relative effectiveness of different forms of housing management in Wales*, HMSO.

Welsh Womens' Aid (1986) *The answer is may be . . . and that's final*! A report about how local authorities in Wales respond to the housing needs of women leaving violent homes with comments and recommendations, WWA.

Wheeler, R. (1985) *Don't Move: we've got you covered: A study of Anchor Housing Trust Staying Put Scheme*, Institute of Housing.

Williams, B. and Mountford-Smith, P. (1989) *Empty Property Owned by Housing Associations in London*, Empty Property Unit.

Williams, G. (1986) *Meeting the Housing Needs of the Elderly: Private initiative or public responsibility*? Occasional Paper No. 17, Department of Town and Country Planning, University of Manchester.

Willmott, P. and Murie, A. (1988) *Polarisation and Social Housing*, Policy Studies Institute.
Widening the Choice: The Next Steps in Housing. (1973) White Paper Cmnd. 5280, London.
Windle, K., Cole, I. and Arnold, P. (1988) *Research Working Papers 1–5*, Housing Decentralisation Research Project, Sheffield City Polytechnic.
Windle, K., Arnold, P. and Cole, I. (1988) *Decentralisation of Housing Services — Structure and process*, Research Working Paper No. 2, Sheffield City Polytechnic.
Women's Aid Federation England (1981) *Leaving Violent Men.*

Index